S0-BXH-548

AMERICAN
POPULAR
PSYCHOLOGY

GARLAND REFERENCE LIBRARY
OF SOCIAL SCIENCE
VOL. 785

AMERICAN POPULAR PSYCHOLOGY

An Interdisciplinary Research Guide

Stephen B. Fried

BF
108
.F75x
1994
West

GARLAND PUBLISHING, INC.
New York & London / 1994

Copyright © 1994 Stephen B. Fried
All rights reserved

Library of Congress Cataloging-in-Publication Data

Fried, Stephen.
American popular psychology : an interdisciplin-
ary research guide / Stephen B. Fried.
    p.   cm — (Garland reference library of social
science ; v. 785)
    Includes indexes.
    ISBN 0-8153-0402-1 (alk. paper)
    1. Psychology—United States—History—Biblio-
graphy.   2. Psychology—Popular works—History—
Bibliography.   3. Psychological literature—United
States—History—Bibliography.   4. Popular culture—
United States—History—Bibliography.   I. Title
II. Title: Popular psychology.   III. Series: Garland
reference library of social science ; v. 785.
Z7204.H57F75   1994
[BF108]
016.15'0973—dc20   94-13412
                                                      CIP

Printed on acid-free, 250-year-life paper
Manufactured in the United States of America

To Connie

Contents

Acknowledgments

This book would not have been possible without the assistance of many persons and institutions. This present work was, in large part, the idea of my former colleague, Dr. Theodore Albrecht. Professor Albrecht, who is now at Kent State University, suggested that I might wish to develop a research guide in the area of popular psychology. Even though he is a musicologist, Ted is in many ways my academic role model, for he is a fine teacher and a superb scholar.

G. Ann Schultis, reference librarian at Park College, prepared the indexes for this book. In addition, Ann located numerous sources, secured those works through interlibrary loan, and reviewed the entire manuscript. Currently, Ann and I are collaborating on a consumer's guide to popular psychology. Ann Schultis is an outstanding librarian who knows how to find and disseminate information in a most effective manner.

Dr. Ronald Miriani, Professor of History at Park College, read and commented on most of the manuscript. Ron's analytic and writing acumen helped to improve the quality of the present work.

Camille Lloyd typed the entire manuscript in a highly professional and timely manner. I appreciate her word-processing skills and thoroughly enjoy working with her.

My friend and colleague, Dr. G. Mack Winholtz, Professor of Sociology at Park College, has reinforced my scholarly efforts and has served as my confidant on academic matters. Mack's quiet grace and sense of order help to center my creative bent.

I started this book during a sabbatical leave in the fall of 1990. The administration of Park College has continued to be supportive of my scholarship, and I have been granted two Faculty Development Awards for my activities. Students in my seminar on the history of popular psychology have aided in the development of the research guide. Sharon Barfield co-wrote the paper on recent self-help bestsellers, which appears as Appendix 3. We presented an earlier version of the paper to the Fifteenth Annual Meeting of the American Culture Association, New Orleans, Louisiana, April 9, 1993. Cia Crawford-Malcolm prepared a draft of the glossary. I also wish to thank Carla Edwards, Tina Girvin, and Wilma Pliley for their various contributions to our study of popular psychology.

Kurt Fried, my oldest child and a junior English major at Washington University (Missouri), tracked down a number of details and copyedited the entire manuscript. I thank Kurt for his continuing interest and encouragement of my scholarly pursuits. Kurt and my daughters, Kim and Katie, have provided much joy over the years.

Several other persons should be noted. Dr. Roger Chatten, Donna Denslow, and Karen Houchins have supported my professional activities in countless ways, and I am grateful to them. Barbara Karni, my editor on a previous book, taught me a great deal about the importance of clarity in writing. Marie Ellen Larcada and Phyllis Korper, my editors at Garland, have been helpful throughout the process of developing the research guide.

Several college and university libraries were used in the preparation of this work. Especially helpful were libraries at the following institutions: University of Iowa, University of Kansas, University of Missouri, Central

Michigan University, Washington University, and Park College.

ᵢ All of the persons and institutions so far mentioned were very important in the development of this work. However, my largest share of gratitude must be given to Connie Boswell, my wife and best friend. A gifted and disciplined landscape painter, Connie helps to create an emotional environment in which scholarship and art are nurtured. Because of some physical limitations, I call on Connie to visit libraries with me, attend conferences, and run a host of errands, all of which take her away from her acrylic knife painting. I truly love my time with Connie, have enormous respect for her artistic creations and self-discipline, and share with her a rather broad sense of humor. I dedicate this book to Connie.

Stephen B. Fried
March 1994

Preface

Numerous aspects of American culture suggest a widespread interest in psychological topics among the general public. Frequently contemporary movies, television programs, newspapers, books, workshops, audiotapes, and a host of other media project therapeutic messages concerning love, marriage, parenting, career, addictions of every sort from alcohol to sex to work, and almost every other conceivable problem associated with the human condition. Psychologists, psychiatrists, counselors, ministers, recovering alcoholics, talk-show hosts, and newspaper and magazine columnists proclaim strategies for solving life's personal and interpersonal trials to all who will read or listen to them. These presentations represent popular psychology, which is distinguished from scientific psychology in that it is intended expressly for general consumption.

We Americans take our "pop psychology" very seriously. During the preparation of this book, the beloved host of a Kansas City radio advice show died of an apparent suicide. Dr. Marshall Saper, a psychologist with a reputation for a biting wit and personal privacy, reportedly took his own life on November 3, 1991. Saper, who had a regional following of around 80,000 listeners a week for his daily call-in show, authored three successful self-help books and maintained a private practice. Reaction to Dr. Saper's death ranged from intense sadness to anger to bewilderment among his loyal radio following, and, in response to the dismay of the public, the talk-radio station devoted a number of days and numerous programs to the consolation of the radio audience, many of whose members shared an outpouring of feelings. Not only did the station enlist the services of several well-known local therapists for these broadcasts, but in addition, engaged Joyce Brothers to to participate for an hour by telephone from Peoria, Illinois. Surely, any time an individual, especially a public one, appears to die in such a fashion, it generates conflicting emotions. People called the station for weeks. These listeners "depended" on Marshall Saper. They "knew" him; he was their personal therapist. Many of these mourners listened to Saper for three hours a day, five days a week. Popular psychology and the area's best-known popular psychologist were linked directly with the lives of the listening audience and a great many members of the larger community (*The Kansas City Star*, Monday, November 4, 1991).

Long before the advent of the radio and television psychology of Marshall Saper, Joyce Brothers, John Bradshaw, Oprah Winfrey, and their compatriots and the current potpourri of self-help books devoted to recovery and dysfunctional families, popular psychology captivated the American public. Nineteenth-century audiences could hardly get enough information from lectures, pamphlets, and books aimed at promoting the wonders of mesmerism and phrenology. This book, a research guide to the scholarly examination of American popular psychology, traces developments from the itinerant mesmerists and phrenologists of the early nineteenth century through analyses of the self-help bestsellers and media offerings of the late twentieth century.

American Popular Psychology: An Interdisciplinary Guide is a selective work covering scholarly commentary from 1950-1992. Included in this research guide is an introductory chapter delineating themes in the history of popular psychology, more than 300 annotations covering scholarly and professional articles and books published from 1950-1992, and an afterword addressing suggested areas for additional research. There are also four appendixes comprising a chronology of events in the history of popular psychology, a listing of self-help psychology bestsellers of 1990, 1991, and 1992, a preliminary analysis of recent self-help bestsellers, and a glossary of popular psychology terms, as well as author and subject indexes.

Annotations have been divided into the following subject headings: historical and sociological treatments; famous popularizers; the popularization of schools of psychology; psychology and the press; self-help books; radio and television psychology; psychological testing; children, romance, and the family; popular psychology and women; popular psychology techniques; and critiques of popular psychology. Works were selected for annotation based on their scholarly discussion of popular psychology. Many of the articles and books centered exclusively on a popular topic while others were broader in scope. The questions to be answered were: (1) Would this source cover a subject germane to a scholarly investigation of popular psychology, and (2) Could its reading have the potential to generate researchable notions?

This interdisciplinary effort will, I hope, encourage scholars in psychology, history, journalism, popular culture, and sociology to expand our understanding of the phenomenon of American popular psychology. It would be delightful to hear from readers who are aware of significant citations which have been omitted from the present text. Additionally, I would be so very pleased to hear from scholars who choose to pursue any of my suggestions for research.

Introduction: Themes in the History of American Popular Psychology

In the words of Robert Fuller (1986), "popular psychology refers to those writings specifically addressed to general reading audiences. What distinguishes psychology as popular is thus its overt intention to help individuals symbolize and resolve problems that arise in the context of everyday life" (p. 173). Much of American culture, including popular psychology, has reflected a preoccupation with success. For several hundred years, immigrants have come to the New World seeking a better life, and American popular psychology has endeavored to reinforce the message of personal material success. The quest for success is reflected currently by what Philip Cushman (298) calls the "empty self" (p. 599,) and Cushman contends that an American enterprise, the self-improvement industry comprised of "mainstream psychology, pop psychology, and pop religion" (p. 604), has developed to help alleviate angst and emptiness as well as to generate profits.

Since colonial days, Americans have been advised by clergy and other influential persons on how to strengthen their character in order to maximize the opportunities for success in this life and in the next. Successful businessmen as well as clergy penned advice books aimed at elevating common men and women through precriptions for improving personality by the use of such tactics as positive thinking and interpersonal manipulation. Eighteenth century guides like Cotton Mather's *Bonifacius: Essays to Do Good* (1710) instruct readers so as to prepare them for the next life, while tomes such as Benjamin Franklin's *The Way to Wealth* (1757) offer guidance in the more secular pursuit of worldly rewards.

Promulgated by traveling lecturers, popular psychological notions traversed America with the mesmerist and phrenological movements (Scott, 44). Early nineteenth century audiences might well have been awe-struck by the showmanship and apparent sincerity of self-proclaimed experts who were willing to apply their skills to all who would listen. In good time, the printed words of newspapers, magazines, pamphlets, and books reinforced the messages of the lecturers and aided in the selling of healings and phrenological readings to a public fascinated with the mysteries of the mind (Stern, 55). The firm of Fowler and Wells was so adroit at marketing the utility of phrenology, that phrenology became, for a time, a nation-wide industry (Bakan, 2).

Interestingly, such movements as mesmerism and phrenology predated the actual beginning of American psychology as a discipline. Psychology did not commence formally until late into the nineteenth century with the research and writings of William James, who was a philosopher as well as America's first psychologist (Cotkin, 67). In its desire for an understanding of the motives and behaviors of human beings, the public did not wait for the science of human behavior to make its entrance onto the American intellectual stage.

Mesmerism led the way to the Mind Cure movement with the latter promoting positive thinking as a remedy for emotional, physical, and spiritual maladies (Fuller, 22, 24). Serving in this tradition was the physician-popularizer, George Beard, who convinced a generation of Americans that they suffered a form of psychic fatigue (neurasthenia) brought on by the dizzying degree of change affecting denizens of the late nineteenth century, including the likes of William James and his sibling, Alice (Evans, 74; Rosenberg, 42; Sicherman, 45).

Arguably America's first scientific psychologists, William James and G. Stanley Hall, were also among the country's first "pop" psychologists. Armed with a mountain of intellectual curiosity, James described both spiritual and behavioral phenomena to the educated public. Blessed with an ability to write clearly and elegantly, James penned the still eloquent *Principles of Psychology* (1890). Of the two, James was the more literary, but Hall the more prolific. Ever the organizer and promoter, it was Hall who arranged for Freud and Jung to visit America in 1909, proselytized for the child study movement, and wrote numerous articles for popular magazines covering everything from masturbation to God (Ross, 90).

Numerous members of the first group of American psychologists engaged in promoting psychological ideas and ideologies to the general public. One of the most influential of this group, Hugo Münsterberg, was not even an American. A staunch German nationalist, Münsterberg, was to become the most popular and ultimately most hated psychologist of his generation. As a Harvard professor, Münsterberg wrote countless articles and books directed squarely at the public fascination with psychology. His popular works covered forensics, film criticism, psychotherapy, investing, and spiritualism, and he became an often-quoted skeptic of a variety of parapsychological phenomena. A powerful political adviser, Münsterberg's German nationalism appeared extreme, and subsequently, he was vilified by the American press and accused of being the Kaiser's spy (Hale, 77; Moskowitz, 89).

Other late nineteenth- and early-twentieth century psychologists engaged in the popularization of their science. Prominent figures like Joseph Jastrow and James McKeen Cattell disseminated behavioral science in large part to further the development of an applied psychology as well as their own careers (Napoli, 39; Sokal, 48, 93).

With the Clark Conference of 1909, psychoanalysis came to America, and by 1915, this brand of therapy was discussed more than any other in the popular magazines (Green & Rieber, 103; Hale, 105; Matthews, 108). It became more and more chic for the intelligentsia to be analyzed; it was the thing to do. Even Edwin Boring, the staunch Harvard experimentalist, underwent analysis, ostensibly to test its efficacy but more likely to combat a debilitating depression. Both highbrows and middle brows were speaking of defense mechanisms, Oedipal longings, and the like (Burnham, 98). To the present day, many lay persons equate psychology with psychoanalysis.

While psychoanalysis was being promoted to an eager public, American experimentalists were developing behaviorism, an environmental and empirical approach to psychological phenomena. Laboratory-based behaviorism's first champion was a most debonair and opinionated student of science, John Broadus Watson. Removing him- self from the academia after a messy divorce, Watson dedicated himself to a career as both applied psychologist and popularizer of behavioristic tenets. Author of the most popular child care guide of his day as well as numerous magazine articles, Watson developed strict guidelines for effective parenting (e.g., he warned against the dangers inherent in too much love from a mother), interpersonal relationships, and business success. With Watson's preachings, popular psychology thus provided a truly American counterpoint to the proclamations of the psychoanalysts (Birnbaum, 111; Buckley 65; Harris, 79; O'Donnell, 115).

At around the same time that Watson was providing an alternative to the psychoanalysts, applied psychologists were occupied with other matters as well. With America entering World War I, a practical need arose regarding personnel selection, intelligence, and the Army. Drawing on his professional activities for the Army, psychologist Robert Yerkes (1923) told *Atlantic Monthly* readers that there were clearly differences between the intellectual levels of the races. Some social scientists who ascribed to such differences argued on behalf of both eugenics and discriminatory immigration policies (Satariano, 155). In 1922 and 1923, the journalist Walter Lippmann wrote a series of articles for the *New Republic* criticizing the analysis of the Army tests by Yerkes, Lewis Terman, and other mainstream American psychologists. Terman, who was to become President of the American Psychological Association, believed that about half of the Army recruits were "morons" with a mental age of less than thirteen. Lippmann presented a logical argument, stressing the impossibility of an "average" person displaying below-average intelligence and arguing that the intelligence tests were designed so that on purely an arbitrary basis, not on raw intelligence, draftees were classified into five categories (Leahey, 32). As a result of the widespread utilization of mental testing in World War I, psychological tests gained a longstanding credibility with the general populace (Leahey, 32; Napoli, 39).

William Leuchtenberg (35) suggests that following World War I, "psychology became a national mania" (p. 164). One of the profession's leading figures, Joseph Jastrow, provided advice through a column, which appeared in over one hundred and fifty newspapers (Schultz and Schultz, 43). Psychology's immense popularity may have reflected what Burnham (11) views as an aspect of the self-indulgence of the Jazz Age, what the author terms a "cult of the self." Critics, such as the humorist Stephen

Leacock and the psychologist Grace Adams, who was to become a popularizer in her own right, were quite vocal about the excesses of the psychology and the gullibility of the general public (Leahey, 32).

During the 1930's and 1940's, psychologists, clergy, and celebrities as well as journalists continued to popularize psychology. Two of the best-selling self-help books of all time were written by a layman, Dale Carnegie (1937), and a pediatrician/psychiatrist, Benjamin Spock (1946). Clearly sales of *How to Win Friends and Influence People* and *Baby and Child Care*, while fulfilling needs of the public, were helped along by the development of the paperback book (Davis, 175).

Popular treatments of psychological topics showed a decline during and following World War II (Burnham, 12). The general public continued to digest a varying quality of material concerning psychopathology and psychotherapy, and popularizers of the day warned a gullible public about the dangers of heeding the advice of quacks and pseudo-scientists (Burnham, 12). During the 1950's, a pop theology reminiscent of the New Thought school was reflected in the works of Norman Vincent Peale.

With the 1960's, a third major school of psychology, a humanistic one (the others being behaviorism and psychoanalysis), was disseminated to the American public (Back, 118, 119, 1987; Lasch, 301; Schur, 306). Through a variety of media, word of the Awareness Movement spread, and it became fashionable in educational, religious, and psychotherapeutic circles to focus on the here-and-now, "feelings," active listening, the entire spectrum of human growth and potential. Among members of the educated public, T-groups, encounter, and Gestalt exercises were marked with the aim of maximizing the possibility of personal actualization (Back, 118).

The 1960's and 1970's saw an outpouring of popular books on humanistic and self-oriented subjects such as Transactional Analysis, Gestalt, Primal therapy, sexuality, Psycho-cybernetics, and self-actualization (Starker, 191). One of the most popular approaches, Transactional Analysis, was formulated by psychiatrists Eric Berne and Thomas Harris as a pedestrian combination of psychoanalysis and interpersonal communication theory. Popular psychology books appeared to become even more self-oriented with emphasis on being *How to be Your Own Best Friend* (Newman and Berkowitz, 1974) and *Looking Out for #1* (Ringer, 1977).

As part of a growing interest in self-awareness and self-expression in the 1960's and 1970's, Americans were provided with numerous self-help books and articles on sexuality (Ehrenreich, Hess, and Jacobs, 266; Simonds, 272). Beginning with works of Masters and Johnson, David Reuben, and Alex Comfort, popularizers discovered a tremendous public curiosity about erotic matters. Far from representing a balanced view of human sexuality, a number of self-help books portray sex in a male-oriented fashion (Simonds, 272). More balanced perspectives began to emerge with the work of the Boston Women's Health Collective in *Our Bodies, Ourselves* in 1971 and in Irene Kassorla's *Nice Girls Do* (1980). Many readers in their quest for the ultimate sexual experience learned of "G spots" (Ladas, Whipple, and Perry, 1982) and "psychasms" (Pearsall, 1987).

Another popular development of the past twenty years has been the radio call-in program featuring psychologists. Dating back at least to the broadcasts of Toni Grant in the early 1970's in Los Angeles, radio psychology has become a big enterprise (Bouhoutsos, Goodchilds, and Huddy, 193). Although many members of the psychological profession voice concerns over media psychology, particularly radio psychology, there is some evidence that radio psychology may well be functioning as a rather effective form of community intervention (Schwebel, 204). An outgrowth of the radio call-in format, the television talk-show program, hosted by persons such as Oprah Winfrey and Phil Donahue, often features persons with apparent psychological/behavioral disorders as well as a therapist who has recently published a book on a related topic. Apparently, the efficacy of this type of format as a community psychology intervention has yet to be put to the empirical test. Certainly the entertainment (or voyeuristic) value is reflected by the enormous ratings which these shows receive.

Criticism of popular psychology has come from many different voices. Psychologists have lambasted their peers as well as journalists for communicating half-truths and generally misinforming an unenlightened public (Rosen, 1981; Rosen, 1987). Psychologists and their work have often been misrepresented in the popular press (Benjamin, 130; Dennis, 134; Satariano, 155). Both journalists and psychologists, recognizing the differing missions of the two professions, have provided suggestions for psychologists and other behavioral scientists when their research and expertise is about to be popularized (Blakeslee, 133; Goldstein, 141; McCall, 145; McCall and Stocking, 146; Stocking and Dunwoody, 159).

Steven Starker (191) concludes his comprehensive analysis of psychological self-help books with some specific conclusions, including a finding from his own research (Starker, 190; 192) that a great many professional psychologists are quite favorably disposed to many popular psychology books, even prescribing them to their clients. Starker contends that those popular works providing specific strategies for personal change could be evaluated empirically, but that such research rarely is undertaken. Apparently, a great many consumers perceive the helpfulness of many of these books even in the absence of any concrete supporting evidence (Simonds, 272; Starker, 191).

American
Popular
Psychology

Historical and Sociological Treatments

This section covers scholarly sources on general historical and social analyses of relevant popular psychological and religious movements. Scholarship from the disciplines of psychology, sociology, history, popular culture, and American studies is included. Annotations include: success literature, popular theology, phrenology, mesmerism, Mind Cure, popular psychology and spiritualism, popular psychology and pseudoscience, neurasthenia, popular psychology in the Progressive Era, and emotion in America.

1.   Anker, R. (1982). Religion and self-help, In M.
     Thomas Inge (Ed.), *Concise histories of
     American popular culture* (pp. 328-345).
     Westport, Connecticut: Greenwood Press.
     This chapter chronicles popular religious
     messages which promote self-help, success, hard
     work, and, ultimately self-responsibility. Attention
     is paid to the inspirational and psychological
     teachings of such New Thought groups as
     Christian Science and Unity. The author mentions
     that popular psychology influenced the bestsellers
     of Rabbi Joshua Liebman and of the liberal
     Protestant, Henry Emerson Fosdick. Included is a
     brief description of the message of a more recent
     self-help preacher, Robert Schuller, who appears
     weekly on television from his "Crystal Cathedral."

2.   Bakan, D. (1966). The influence of phrenology
     on American psychology, *Journal of the
     History of the Behavioral Sciences*, 2, 200-
     220.
     The author argues that phrenology had a
     great impact on the development of psychology in
     America. In the mid-nineteenth century, phren-
     ology was debated at such universities as Harvard,
     Cornell, and Missouri, and many leading figures,
     such as Walt Whitman and Horace Mann, had
     themselves phrenologized. In part, the popular-
     ization of phrenology was due to successful
     marketing by the firm of Fowler and Wells, which,
     through lecture tours and publications, made
     phrenology a nation-wide industry.

3.   Bakan, D. (1977). Political factors in the
     development of American psychology,

Annals of the New York Academy of Sciences, 291, 221-232.
Entertaining essay which describes differences between the dominant psychology of the academy with that of the larger culture. Makes a case for the role of fiction writers in fostering a Freudian point of view in American society.

4. Bakan, D. (1980). Politics and American psychology, in R.W. Rieber and Kurt Salzinger (Eds.), *Psychology: Theoretical-historical perspectives*, (pp. 125-144). New York: Academic Press.
Rambling essay which contains several allusions to the popularization of psychology, including comments on the Americanization of psychoanalysis as well as on baby-boomers and Skinner's Air-Crib.

5. Baumeister, R.F. (1986). *Identity: Cultural change and the struggle for self.* N.Y.: Oxford University Press.
Examines issues surrounding self-identity from socio-historical and psychological viewpoints. Topics include brief treatments of identity in medieval, early modern, and modern contexts, identity and adolescence, and the nature of identity. The author comments on the appeal of popular psychological tomes as a promise of self-fulfillment.

6. Bellah, R., Madsen, R., Sullivan, W., Swidler, A., and Tipton, S. (1985). *Habits of the heart: Individualism and commitment in American*

life. Berkeley: University of California Press.

American mores are dissected in this compassionate sociological examination. As a form of popular discourse in the late nineteenth and early twentieth centuries, psychology is viewed as contributing to what the authors term "expressive individualism." In the chapter of the book entitled, "Reaching Out," Bellah and associates describe therapy and therapeutic langauge as synonymous with late twentieth century American middle class values and social practice. In this chapter there is an insightful section on "American nervousness" of the nineteenth and twentieth century including a discussion of William James and his "gospel of relaxation," which fits into the combined tradition of spirituality and popular psychology. A society that elevates the therapeutic relationship as a model for all relationships, in a sense, elevates the self and self-concern as the ultimate interest. Bellah and his colleagues wrestle with forces that lead us toward community versus those pressures that send us back to self.

7. Benjamin, L.T. (1986). Why don't they understand us? A history of psychology's public image. *American Psychologist*, 41, 941-946.

Included in this paper is a description of the development of the discipline's public image in America. Beginning with the establishment of experimental laboratories in the late 1880's and concluding with comments on psychology and World War II, the author emphasizes the relationship between socioeconomic conditions and psychology's public image. The paper includes sections labelled: "Venturing Beyond Academe," "Psychology and the Popular Press," and "Postwar Popularity."

8. Benjamin Jr., L. (1993). *A history of psychology in letters*. Dubuque, IA: Brown & Benchmark.

   This delightful little book contains a sample of correspondence of a number of prominent philosophers and psychologists from John Locke through Abraham Maslow. Each chapter includes a brief introductory essay, passages from letters, and an annotated bibliography. The annotated bibliographies on Cattell, James, Watson, Freud, and Skinner are quite useful.

9. Bode, C. (1956). *The American lyceum: Town meeting of the mind.* New York: Oxford University Press.

   Devotes a section to George Combe's American lectures on phrenology, which began in 1838.

10. Boring, E. (1950). *A history of experimental psychology* (2nd edition). Englewood Cliffs, NJ: Prentice-Hall.

    This text is essential reading for anyone with a serious interest in the history of psychology. I first learned about the links between phrenology and psychology when I read the third chapter of this book as an undergraduate in the late 1960's.

11. Burnham, J. (1968). The new psychology: From narcissism to social control, in John Braeman, Robert Bremner, and David Brody (Eds.), *Change and continuity in twentieth century America: The 1920's*, (pp. 351-398). Columbus: Ohio State University Press. Portrays the new psychology of the 1920's as reflecting the self-indulgence of the Jazz Age. Psychological principles were frequently sensationalized and oversimplified. Popular versions of psychoanalysis, glandular conceptions of personality, autosuggestion, and behaviorism were definite aspects of the Zeitgeist. Confessional newspaper columns and magazines flourished during this period and may have reflected a "cult of the self."

12. Burnham, J. (1987). *How superstition won and lost: Popularizing science and health in the United States*. New Brunswick, NJ: Rutgers University Press. In the third chapter of this seminal book on the popularization of American science and health, social historian Burnham provides an analysis of psychology's path from the nineteenth century to the present. The author describes media for the diffusion of psychological notions, including lecture tours and mass-circulation newspapers and magazines, and radio. Included in a chapter on psychology are discussions of phrenology, mesmerism, experimental psychology, popular textbooks, pop journals from *Practical Psychology* (1900-1902) to *Psychology Today*, professional psychological popularizers from Münsterberg to

Watson, and the development of the American Psychological Association as an institution of popularization. Burnham suggests that the psychology of the nineteenth-century was "common property among educated people" (p. 85), and he argues that twentieth-century psychology followed a pattern of popularization, dilution, and trivialization. Perhaps this is the best available synthesis of the history of popular psychology.

13. Carlson, E., & Simpson, M. (1970). Perkinism vs. mesmerism, *Journal of the History of the Behavioral Sciences*, 6, 16-24.

Perkinism, which was similar to mesmerism, was a psychophysical treatment developed by Dr. Elisha Perkins at the end of the eighteenth-century. Among Perkins' supporters was Samuel Magaw, the secretary of the American Philosophical Society. Like mesmerism, Perkinism was discredited, which culminated in the expulsion of Perkins from the Connecticut Medical Society in 1796. A major proponent of Perkinism was the founder's son, Benjamin, who published and lectured widely in America and in England.

14. Cawelti, J. (1965). *Apostles of the self-made man.* Chicago: University of Chicago Press.

Describes the image of the self-made man as reflecting a middle-class Protestant ethic, economic advancement, fulfillment, and social progress, with the latter two themes rarely reflected in the popular literature. Much of the gospel of self-help, while advocating discipline as the road to wealth, sought to preserve the existing social order. Typically, nineteenth-century handbooks proclaimed the true worth of the common man who worked hard. There were important critics of the gospel of the self-made man, notably figures like the historian Francis Parkman and the novelist, James Fenimore Cooper, who saw a necessity for a cultured upper class, a part of which the commoner could never be. Most of the book is devoted to a treatment of such twentieth-century popularizers as Norman Vincent Peale, Dale Carnegie, and Napoleon Hill.

15. Coon, D. (1992). Testing the limits of sense and science: American experimental psychologists combat spiritualism, 1880-1920, *American Psychologist*, 47, 143-151.

Discusses the conflicts that spiritualism presented as psychologists attempted to forge an experimental science which would ascend to its rightful place alongside the existing empirical disciplines. Most psychologists sought to disassociate themselves from any connection with spiritualism, while others attempted to examine the claims of psychics and mediums according to scientific method. Spiritualism held enormous popular appeal and was linked to psychology by much of the public. By examining the claims of spiritualism, psychologists were able to respond to public interest as well as to establish themselves as experts on mental issues. Popularizing psychologists, like Hugo Münsterberg and Joseph Jastrow, wrote about related topics in the pages of such magazines as *Atlantic Monthly* and *Popular Science Monthly*.

16. Cravens, H., & Burnham, J. (1971). Psychology and evolutionary naturalism in American

thought, 1890-1940, *American Quarterly*, 23, 635-657. Includes a number of comments about popular presentations of psychological views on evolutionary concepts. For example, psychology's misuse of the white rat was a common theme of the 1930's. In a footnote, Cravens and Burnham state: "Popularization of psychology generally followed main trends within the discipline itself" (p. 651).

17. Curti, M. (1980). *Human nature in American thought: A history.* Madison: The University of Wisconsin Press.
    Through an analysis of American intellectual and popular writings, the author carves a history of views of human nature in the New World. Particularly apropos arc chapters on "The Emerging Science of Human Nature," "Nature versus Nurture," "Exploring the Unconscious," and "The Behavioral Movement." The author argues that both positive and negative views of human nature were reinforced by the opportunities and the struggles of American life.

18. Dain, N. (1964). *Concepts of insanity in the United States, 1789-1865.* New Brunswick, NJ: Rutgers University Press.
    The author devotes two entire chapters to opinions about mental illness as expressed through the popular media of the day. Two of the most popular books from the earlier years were William Buchan's *Domestic Medicine* and John Wesley's *Primitive Physic*, with the former taking a

psychological approach while the latter took a decidedly more commonsense path. Eighteenth-century newspaper accounts often sensationalized the horrible nature of various crimes purported to have been carried out by insane perpetrators. By the middle of the nineteenth century, public opinion had moved toward more acceptance of humane treatment of those afflicted with mental illness. However, there continued to be concern with the medical care of the day as witnessed by the lectures, pamphlets, and books offered by disgruntled former psychiatric patients who decried the care received in psychiatric institutions. Newspaper accounts often reinforced these charges, while magazine writers were less inclined to fuel the criticisms. Dain suggests that "The public concept of insanity remained generally vague and amorphous throughout the pre-Civil War period" (p. 202).

19. Dallenbach, K. (1955). Phrenology versus psychoanalysis, *American Journal of Psychology*, 68, 511-525.
    Dallenbach sees similarities between the development of phrenology and that of psychoanalysis. Includes a brief section on the popularization of phrenology.

20. Degler, C. (1991). *In search of human nature: The decline and revival of Darwinism in American social thought.* New York: Oxford University Press.
    Describes biological views of human behavior articulated by American social scientists. Includes discussions of the popularization of early nineteenth-century arguments in favor of eugenic

and restrictive immigration policies and a brief description of popular treatments of ethological themes beginning in the 1960's by Konrad Lorenz, Desmond Morris, and playwright Robert Ardrey.

21. Fancher, R. (1979). *Pioneers of psychology*. New York: Norton.

Based upon a personalistic view of the history of psychology, this volume includes a lengthy discussion of some of the key figures in the phrenological movement. Also, there is a description of phrenology's predecessor in popular psychology, physiognomy, which relied upon physical features as the basis of individual character.

22. Fuller, R. (1986). *Americans and the unconscious*. New York: Oxford University Press.

In this text, the author follows the development of the notion of the unconscious in American religious and psychological thought. Beginning with a discussion of theological anticipations of the unconscious, Fuller describes mesmerism, the early functionalist psychologists, the introduction of psychoanalytic thinking into American thought, the relationship between behaviorism and the unconscious, humanistic psychology and the rediscovery of psychology, and a final chapter titled, "The Apotheosis: The Unconscious in Popular Psychology." This last chapter includes what may be the clearest definition of popular psychology in print. According to Fuller, "popular psychology refers to those writings specifically addressed to general reading audiences. What distinguishes a psychology as popular is thus its overt intention to help

individuals symbolize and resolve problems that
arise in the context of everyday life" (p. 173).

23. Fuller, R. (1982). Carl Rogers, religion, and the
role of psychology in American culture,
Journal of Humanistic Psychology, 22, 21-
32.
The author disagrees with critics of
American psychology who believe that its
teachings are responsible for some of the ills of
contemporary society. In making his argument,
Fuller draws comparisons between Rogers and
Freud and claims that "academe notwithstanding,
Freudian thought has by and large failed to filter
into the stock of ideas from which Americans take
their bearings on life" (p. 24). In contrast, the
author asserts that the teachings of Rogers have
been far more accessible to the general public and
"more congenial to the melioristic temperament of
American society during the 1950's and 1960's"
(p. 24). In addition, the author believes that the
teachings of Rogers have kinship with those of
Jonathan Edwards, Ralph Waldo Emerson, and
William James with their emphasis on self-reliance
and that the notion of self-actualization does not
lead to narcissism but rather to a deeper
spirituality.

24. Fuller, R. (1982). *Mesmerism and the American
cure of souls*. Philadelphia: University of
Pennsylvania Press.
Exceptional treatment of mesmerism's role
in the development of American popular psychology. Asserts that the mesmerists "were the first
to popularize psychological ideas as a resource for

religious self-understanding" (p. 183). Chapters of note are entitled "The Emergence of an American Psychology," "Psychology out of Its Mind," and "Psychology as Popular Philosophy."

25. Henry, L., Jr. (1981). Unorthodox science as a popular activity, *Journal of American Culture*, 4, 1-22.

Unorthodox scientists who may attempt to uncover "secrets of the universe" often demonstrate imagination, persistence, and resourcefulness. Many of us schooled in orthodox science find it tempting to condescend toward those who practice this form of popularization. This essay includes a brief discussion of the renegade psychiatrist, Wilhelm Reich, and his discovery, the orgone.

26. Hilgard, E. (1987). *Psychology in America: A historical survey.* San Diego: Harcourt Brace Jovanovich.

Comprehensive yet readable, this text centers on the science and profession of psychology. A number of passages address popularization. For example, in a chapter devoted to the rise of developmental psychology, Hilgard describes the child study movement of the late nineteenth and early twentieth centuries and includes comments on L. Emmett Holt's popular guide of 1894, *The Care and Feeding of Children.*

27. Hilgard, E., Leary, D., & McGuire, G. (1991). History of psychology: A survey and critical assessment, *Annual Review of Psychology*, 42, 79-107.

Introductory review of the historiography of psychology. A section entitled "Internalism vs Externalism" includes a brief discussion of scholarship which connects psychology with other aspects of culture and society.

28. Holifield, E. (1983). *A history of pastoral care in America: From salvation to self-realization.* Nashville: Abingdon Press.

This solid historical treatment chronicles the development of pastoral care from the seventeenth century through the 1960's. The focus of pastoral counseling evolved from the saving of souls to an emphasis on the realization of self. Developments in the social sciences, especially psychology, impacted both the message and style of American clergy. Devotes an entire section to American popular psychology and suggests that, after World War II, pop psychology contributed to an expanded interest in pastoral care.

29. Huber, R. (1971). *The American idea of success.* New York: McGraw-Hill.

Traces success-oriented self-help literature from Franklin to Peale. A chapter entitled "Day by Day, in Every Way, I Am Getting Better and Better" describes reformulations of Coué's autosuggestion that were promoted as applied psychology during the 1920's. Huber states that: "Psychoanalysts like Freud, Jung, and Adler soon had self-helpsters peering into the subconscious for clues to success" (p. 179). One enterprising business, the Psycho-Phone Company, offered a foolproof technique for autosuggestion while the customer slept. Similar forms of mind power, still being sold in the 1990's, continue despite a vacuum of empirical support attesting to their efficacy. One of the strengths of Huber's work is a comprehensive primary and secondary bibliography.

30. Jerison, H. (1977). Should phrenology be rediscovered?, *Current Anthropology*, 18, 744-746.
    Describes some of the contributions of Franz Joseph Gall to the bio-behavioral sciences. Cautions against "swallowing" the whole package of popular phrenology.

31. Karier, C. (1986). *Scientists of the mind: Intellectual founders of modern psychology*, Urbana: University of Illinois Press.
    The author argues that with the rise of secularism in American society, psychology came to assume the role of defining human nature, which was previously held by theology and philosophy. This theme is evident in such chapters as "William James: Religion and the Rise of the Therapeutic Society" and "G. Stanley Hall: Priestly Prophet of a New Dispensation." The book is a biographical study of some of the key figures who created "the major movements of the psychological society during its critical, formative period from 1890 to 1910" (p. 14). Karier sees clear links between religious and psychological practice. For example, he likens Erhard's est or attack therapy to the harangues of Jonathan Edwards, and he views Watson's behaviorism as clearly connected with the psychologist's early religious upbringing.

32.   Leahey, T. (1991).   *A history of modern psychology*. Englewood Cliffs, NJ: Prentice-Hall.
      This book is one of a handful covering the history of psychology while including popular ramifications. Especially illuminating are the chapter covering early applied psychology, the section concerning "psychology's occult doubles," and the material on "giving psychology away." In closing the book, the author argues that: "The Me Decade, the Me Society, was the nearly inevitable result of scientism and psychology" (p. 395).

33.   Leahey, T. & Leahey, G. (1983).   *Psychology's occult doubles: Psychology and the problem of pseudoscience*. Chicago: Nelson-Hall.
      Psychologists have often derided the so-called pseudosciences of parapsychology, phrenology, mesmerism, and spiritualism. These "occult doubles" of psychology offer explanations that are not altogether consistent with a naturalistic world view. The Leaheys argue that these occult systems have arisen in order to promote various religious and moral values. For example, a chapter covering "contemporary therapeutic cults" includes a thorough discussion of Scientology is described as a relatively complex form of faculty psychology, which views itself as a religion. Concludes that various pseudosciences arise to offer answers to questions that science does not provide.

34.   Lears, T. (1983).   From salvation to self-realization: Advertising and the therapeutic roots of the consumer culture, 1880-1930. In Richard Wightman Fox and T. Jackson

Lears (Eds.) *The culture of consumption: Critical essays in American history 1880-1980* (pp. 1-38). New York: Pantheon Books.

Describes "the emergence of a therapeutic ethos" (p. 6-17). Psychologists like James and Hall, even though invoking religious images and ideals, moved America in a secular direction. During the years under scrutiny, "an emphasis on the sanctity of human potential led to a new definition of religion" (p. 14). A number of prominent religious figures redefined American Protestantism as a kind of "abundance therapy" (p. 14). Experience became an end in itself, contributing to "therapeutic advertising" (p. 19), which evolved into social control. Psychologists Walter Dill Scott and J. B. Watson were central players in these therapeutic enterprises. Lears utilizes the career of Bruce Barton, co-founder of a highly successful advertising agency and author of a plethora of inspirational articles and books, to illustrate the merging of the therapeutic ethos with consumer culture.

35. Leuchtenburg, W. (1958). *The perils of prosperity, 1914-32*. Chicago: The University of Chicago Press.

Well-written social history that includes a chapter, "The Revolution in Morals," a thoughtful discussion of behaviorism, Freudian influences, and sex. Suggests that after World War I, "psychology became a national mania" (p. 164). Argues that the popularity of Freud's ideas had a profound impact on American morals. Leuchtenburg claims that many Americans believed that Freud "shared the American conviction that every man had the right not merely to pursue happiness but to possess it." (p. 166). Many of the taboos surrounding sexuality dissipated.

36. Meyer, D. (1980). *The positive thinkers: Religion as pop psychology from Mary Baker Eddy to Oral Roberts.* New York: Pantheon Books.

This book traces the "psychologizing" of American religious thought and practice. Mind cures first took hold in off-shoot Protestant sects like Christian Science and Unity but eventually came to be interwoven in the old-line Protestant churches as reflected in the teachings of Norman Vincent Peale. The author contends that Americans had need of a theology sprinkled with psychology in order to combat their general sense of anxiety and to gain control of their lives.

37. Miller, G. (1969). Psychology as a means of promoting human welfare, *American Psychologist*, 24, 1063-1075.

In his presidential address to the American Psychological Association, Miller challenges psychologists to do everything in their power "to give psychology away." Representative of Miller's directive are the following words:

> I believe that part of the answer is that psychology must be practiced by nonpsychologists. We are not physicians; the secrets of our trade need not be reserved for highly trained specialists. Psychological facts should be passed out freely to all who need and can use them"
> (p. 1070).

In this way, Miller sees the complete popularization of psychology as the coming mission of psychologists.

38. Morawski, J. (1988). Impossible experiments and practical constructions: The social bases of psychologists' work, in Jill Morawski (Ed.), *The rise of experimentation in American psychology* (pp. 72-93). New Haven: Yale University Press.

Describes examples from the period covering 1910 to 1940 of how social factors impacted the decisions of research psychologists, regarding topic, variables, methodology as well as experimental subjects. Includes discussion of sex differences, mental testing, and infrahumans and comments on some popular efforts by such notables as G. S. Hall, J. B. Watson, and B. F. Skinner.

39. Napoli, D. (1981). *Architects of adjustment: The history of the psychological profession in the United States.* Port Washington, NY: Kennikat Press.

Describes the profession of psychology as a servant of the status quo. By focusing on adjustment, psychologists have often reinforced the existing social order. In a chapter entitled "The Perils of Popularity," the author recalls humorist Stephen Leacock who wrote that America was "suffering from 'an outbreak of psychology'." Napoli reflects that Sears Roebuck began marketing Freud and speculates on the reasons for psychology's decline during the Depression.

40. Parker, G. (1973). *Mind Cure in New England:*
     From the Civil War to World War I.
     Hanover, NH: University Press of New
     England.
         Traces the development of Mind Cure as a
     populist self-help movement. Through a growing
     book and periodical market, many Americans were
     gaining access to the teachings and psychological
     techniques of New Thought. Due to the successes
     of Mind Cure, many Americans were open to the
     notion of the psychological foundation of much
     mental and physical strife, which eased the way for
     acceptance of psychoanalytic principles. Separate
     chapters chronicle the roles of such luminaries as
     Emerson, Eddy, and William James. A seven-page
     bibliographical note describes relevant primary and
     secondary sources.

41. Rieber, R. (1980). The Americanization of
     psychology before William James, in R.W.
     Rieber   and   Kurt   Salzinger   (Eds.),
     Psychology: Theoretical-historical
     perspectives (pp. 103-123). New York:
     Academic Press.
         The main emphasis of this chapter is on
     nineteenth   century   philosopher/psychologist
     Thomas Upham, who offered a compromise
     between free will and determinism. The author
     concludes the chapter with a three-page diatribe on
     the state of present-day psychology. Rieber cites
     a popular article by Christopher Lasch, which
     castigates   the   influence   of   the   "psychiatric
     priesthood." Rieber takes sharp aim at the wider
     American public, writing of:

the powerful and personal appeal of
psychology to the American public.
And if someone packages it and
puts it up for sale, the American
public will buy it. From phrenology
to psychoanalysis, it has experienced
its most dramatic successes and its
most overwhelming influences, in
the marketplace of the mind
(p. 120).

42. Rosenberg, C. (1976). *No other gods: On science
and American social thought.* Baltimore:
The Johns Hopkins University Press.
Well-written description of the relationships
between science and popular culture movements.
Especially noteworthy are chapters on heredity,
sexual role and social class, and George Beard's
views on neurasthenia. Rosenberg claims that
Beard's notions regarding American nervousness
reflect a certain ambivalence "between an
ingeniously arrogant nationalism and a chronic
national insecurity between optimism and
pessimism" (p. 107). Beard had a number of
contemporary critics who viewed him as a self-
promoter, with one neuroanatomist believing Beard
to be "a kind of Barnum of American medicine"
(p. 108). Included is a bibliographic essay, which
leads the reader to numerous valuable secondary
sources.

43. Schultz, D., and Schultz, S. (1992). *A history of
modern psychology* (5th edition). San
Diego: Harcourt Brace Jovanovich.

This lively history of American psychology
includes discussion of the popular notions of
several philosophers and psychologists.   In this
vein, the authors describe Herbert Spencer, who
was lauded as a hero when he arrived in America
from England in 1882.   Spencer was a celebrity
whose

> Works were serialized in popular
> magazines, his books sold hundreds
> of thousands of copies.   Had there
> been television, Spencer would
> doubtless have appeared on talk
> shows.
>
>   (p. 128).

44.   Scott, D. (1980).   The popular lecture and the
      creation of a public in mid-nineteenth-
      century America, *Journal of American
      History*, 66, 791-809.
      During the middle of the nineteenth century,
      public lectures reached large numbers of persons.
      These presentations were open to a wide public
      who typically were charged for admission and, in
      return, were informed and entertained.   Lectures,
      usually delivered by members of the professions or
      intellectuals, were often aimed at diffusing "useful
      knowledge" to the masses.   Many enterprising
      professionals, including the attorney and
      phrenologist Amos Dean, used the public lecture
      for career enhancement.

45.   Sicherman, B. (1977).   The uses of a diagnosis:
      Doctors, patients, and neurasthenia, *Journal*

of the History of Medicine and Allied Sciences, 32, 33-54.
Includes a description of Margaret Cleaves' 1910 book, *The Autobiography of a Neurasthene*, a popular account of this most popular of late nineteenth- and earlier twentieth-century disturbances. Ironically, George Beard, the chief promotor of the diagnostic label of neurasthenia in both medical journals and popular circles, viewed the "periodical press" as one of the key culprits in an ever-growing environment of stress, which placed excess pressure on Americans of his day and contributed to widespread nervous disorders.

46. Smith, J. (1963). The day of the popularizers: The 1920's, *South Atlantic Quarterly*, 62, 297-309.
Describes a number of popular books written by prominent intellectuals. Includes a discussion of George Dorsey's *Why We Behave Like Human Beings*, which appeared in 1925. Unlike many of the popularizers of today, a great number of those who filled that role in the 1920's were true scholars.

47. Sokal, M. (Ed.) (1981). *An education in psychology: James McKeen Cattell's journal and letters from Germany and England, 1880-1888.* Cambridge, MA: The MIT Press.
Includes 455 documents penned by the popularizer and future editor of *Science, Popular Science Monthly, The Scientific Monthly, The American Naturalist,* and *School and Society.*

Useful postscript contains information on Cattell's subsequent professional life.

48.   Sokal, M. (1981). The origins of the Psychological Corporation, *Journal of the History of the Behavioral Sciences*, 17 (pp. 54-67). The author examines the early years of the Psychological Corporation, a highly successful venture in applied psychology. During the early 1920's, professional psychologists like Cattell were alarmed about the presence of a number of pseudo-scientific movements (e.g., the Blackford School of Character Analysis). In part, the Psychological Corporation was formed in order to set a standard for applied psychology and to protect the public from ubiquitous pseudo-psychologists.

49.   Sokal, M., and Rafail, P. (1982). *A guide to manuscript collections in the history of psychology and related areas*, Millwood, NY: Kraus International Publications. The authors have compiled a description of over five hundred individual manuscript collections as well as a discussion of significant manuscript repositories. There are twelve separate entries regarding phrenology and delineations of the manuscript collections of such popularizers as Louise Ames, Walter Van Dyke Bingham, James McKeen Cattell, Rudolf Dreikurs, G. Stanley Hall, Joseph Jastrow, Hugo Münsterberg, and John Broadus Watson.

50.   Stearns, C., and Stearns, P. (1986). *Anger: The struggle for emotional control in America's*

history. Chicago: The University of Chicago Press.

In summarizing their interdisciplinary history of American anger management, psychiatrist Carol Stearns and historian Peter Stearns emphasize a continued effort to limit the expression of hostility. Maintaining control over anger has been a consistent message in popular advice literature of both the religious and behavioral science varieties. Specific chapters chronicle advice regarding anger in the work setting, in child rearing, and in marriage. Extensive notes provided by the authors suggest a myriad of valuable historical and psychological sources.

51. Stearns, P. (1988). Anger and American work: A twentieth-century turning point, in Carol Stearns and Peter Stearns (Eds.), *Emotion and social change: Toward a new psychohistory* (pp. 123-149). New York: Holmes & Meier.

Describes varied methods of anger control applied to segments of the American workforce. Factory workers have been heavily sanctioned for demonstrations of anger lest these behaviors erupt into violence, while structuring of the sentiments of white-collar workers, though more subtle, continues through popular guidebooks like those of Dale Carnegie as well as management training courses. Stearns describes the use of T-groups in the 1960's as a form of anger control for some management personnel. As an aside, Stearns contends that top executives have been allowed to express anger in whatever fashion they choose.

Perhaps some future empirical research might
confirm or reject such a sweeping hypothesis.

52.   Stearns, P. (1988). The rise of sibling jealousy in
       the twentieth-century, in Carol Stearns and
       Peter Stearns (Eds.), *Emotion and social
       change: Toward a new psychohistory* (pp.
       193-222). New York: Holmes & Meier.
Contends that in nineteenth-century popular
parenting guides little mention is made of sibling
jealousy, but by the 1920's a number of widely-
read tomes offer warnings of the dangers of such
feelings. However, even well into the present
century, some "experts" like the Watsonians
minimized the depth of the problem. Stearns
suggests that during this century there has been "a
significant rise in childhood jealousy" (p. 215), but
this assertion is made despite any introduction of
concrete evidence.

53.   Stearns, P. (1989). Suppressing unpleasant
       emotions: The development of a twentieth-
       century style, In Andrew Barnes and Peter
       Stearns (Eds.), *Social history and issues in
       human consciousness: Some interdiscip-
       linary connections* (pp. 230-261). New
       York: New York University Press.
Traces the development of the management
of anger and jealousy in nineteenth- and twentieth-
century America. Cites popular family manuals
which guided parents in socializing their children
to express or suppress these emotions in a
culturally prescribed fashion.

54. Stearns, P., and Stearns, C. (1985). Emotionology: Clarifying the history of emotions and emotional standards, *American Historical Review*, 90, 813-836.

The Stearns offer the term "emotionology" as a way of differentiating "the collective emotional standards of a society from the emotional experiences of individuals and groups" (p. 813). Certainly advice books emanating from lay and professional writers reflect and promote the "collective emotional standards" of a given era.

55. Stern, M. (1971). *Heads and headlines: The phrenological Fowlers.* Norman, OK: University of Oklahoma Press.

Splendid biography of a family noted for spreading the psychological gospel of phrenology across America. Depicts the Fowlers as radical reformers. Includes a comprehensive listing of primary sources on phrenology.

56. Susman, W. (1984). *Culture as history: the transformation of American society in the twentieth-century.* New York: Pantheon Books.

In this highly readable socio-historical analysis, the author explores threads that connect intellectual themes with those of the popular culture. Most notable is the chapter entitled, "'Personality' and Twentieth-Century Culture," which includes a discussion of self-improvement guides published during the first twenty years of the century. These manuals may attest to a general cultural shift from an emphasis on "character" to "personality."

57.   Walsh, A. (1970).   Is phrenology foolish?   A
      rejoinder,   *Journal   of   the   History   of
      Behavioral Sciences*, 6, 358-361.
           This rejoinder attempts to correct a popular
      article appearing in *Psychology Today*.   Walsh
      laments that the author of the article, David Bakan,
      has failed to consult the necessary primary sources.
      In one of the footnotes, Walsh attributes the
      accuracy problems with the *Psychology Today*
      article as a result of its having been written for a
      popular audience and states that another of Bakan's
      articles (*Journal of the History of the Behavioral
      Sciences*, 2, 200-220, 1966) does not contain as
      many errors as the more popularized version.

58.   Walsh, A. (1971).   George Combe: A portrait of a
      heretofore generally unknown behaviorist,
      *Journal of the History of the Behavioral
      Sciences*, 7, 269-278.
           Clearly one of the shining "heads" of the
      phrenological   movement,   George   Combe
      influenced such nineteenth-century notables as
      Ralph Waldo Emerson, Henry Ward Beecher,
      Edgar Allan Poe, and Horace Mann.   From 1838 to
      1841, Combe lectured widely in the northeastern
      United States.

59.   Wind, J. (1990).   Enemies or fellow travellers?   In
      D. Browning, T. Jobe, and I. Evison (Eds.),
      *Religious and ethical factors in psychiatric
      practice* (pp. 88-106).   Chicago: Nelson-
      Hall.
           Wind suggests that many of the leaders of
      popular religion and psychiatry of the late nine-
      teenth-century coexisted more than they clashed.

Although the mind cure approach of Phineas Quimby and Mary Baker Eddy provided an alternative to the mainstream medical approaches of the day, mind cure set up a clear link between medical therapy and faith. The leaders of the Emmanuel Movement, Samuel McComb and Elwood Worcester, tried to accommodate "the new psychology of modernity and the Christian tradition" (p. 100). By 1910, McComb and Worcester had developed into highly popular lecturers, and their message was touted in such periodicals as *Good Housekeeping* and *Ladies' Home Journal*.

60. Wrobel, A. (1975). Orthodoxy and respectability in nineteenth-century phrenology, *Journal of Popular Culture*, 9, 38-50.

Describes the scientific orientation of many of the early phrenologists who ascribed to Baconian inductive philosophy. Siding with the Scottish commonsense philosophy of Dugald Stewart, Thomas Brown, and Thomas Reid, phrenology viewed the mind as reflective as opposed to the view of empiricists or sensationalists like John Locke, who saw the mind as passive and determined by experience. Phrenology's respectability was reinforced by the many leading nineteenth-century intellectuals who sang its praises. Though rooted in laboratory science, gradually phrenology became more and more practical "as it capitalized on a prevalent enthusiasm for self-culture and self-improvement" (p. 45). States that the lack of formal scientific training of the Fowler brothers, the most successful promoters of phrenology, contributed to its moving more and more into "indiscriminate eclecticism" (p. 46) and the practical applications of individual counseling and headreading.

61. Wrobel, A. (Ed.) (1987). *Pseudo-science and society in nineteenth century America.* Lexington, KY: The University Press of Kentucky.
This volume contains entertaining and thoughtful essays on several pseudo-sciences, which had popular psychological elements. Of particular interest are the chapters by Taylor Stoehr, John Greenway, Harold Aspiz, and Robert Fuller which cover, respectively, phrenologist Robert Collyer, popular electrical treatments for "nervous disease," pseudo-scientific views of sexuality, and mesmerism as the first popular American psychology.

62. Wyllie, I. (1954). *The self-made man in America. The myth of rags to riches.* New Brunswick, NJ: Rutgers University Press.
Chronicles the theme of self-help and the self-made man. Wealthy men like Barnum, Rockefeller, and Carnegie wrote self-congratulatory homilies offering advice while promoting the virtue of success. Some of the titans of free enterprise, like John Jacob Astor, hired publicists to articulate the cult of self-made success. In addition to books and pamphlets, the lecture served as a popular means of disseminating the ideas of success, with Horace Mann and Edward Everett being among the more prominent figures who spoke on the subject.

Wyllie writes that the mass appeal of the message of the success cult "was because it preached simple doctrines to simple men" (p. 123). Can the same be said of the attraction of the self-help message of success articulated in the present era?

Famous Popularizers

This section includes sources covering nineteenth- and twentieth-century American popularizers of psychological notions. These persons communicated with lay audiences through books, articles, and lectures. The popularizing efforts of the following notables are covered in this section: George Beard, James McKean Cattell, Sigmund Freud, Arnold Gesell, G. Stanley Hall, Emmett Holt, Ethel Puffer Howes, William James, Joseph Jastrow, Hugo Münsterberg, Carl Rogers, B. F. Skinner, Benjamin Spock, Lewis Terman, Edward Thorndike, John Broadus Watson, Rosalie Rayner Watson, Robert Sessions Woodworth, and Harry Kirke Wolf.

63. Ames, L. (1989). *Arnold Gesell: Themes of his
     work.* New   York: Human   Sciences
     Press.
     Offers a non-critical description of the
     contributions of the pediatrician and specialist in
     child development. Pertinent sections cover
     Gesell's role in the mental hygiene movement, his
     offerings on parental guidance, and the differences
     between his popular work and that of Benjamin
     Spock.

64. Bach, W. (1974). The influence of psycho-
     analytic thought on Benjamin   Spock's
     "Baby and Child Care," *Journal of the
     History of the Behavioral Sciences,* 10, 91-
     94.
     Argues that Spock's book is psycho-
     analytic in its derivation. Bach comes to the
     defense of Spock against attacks from other
     popularizers like Norman Vincent Peale. This
     paper's sentimentalism and idealism are reflected
     in the statement: "I see the Spock generation as
     caring for us all, and for the world" (p. 93). This
     paper was originally presented in 1972. Were
     psychiatrists and other behavioral scientists more
     idealistic then? Perhaps.

65. Benjamin, Jr., L. T. (1991). *Harry Kirke Wolfe:
     Pioneer in psychology.* Lincoln, NE:
     University of Nebraska Press.
     This biography of the early American
     psychologist describes Wolfe's important role in
     the development of the child study movement.
     Benjamin recounts that it was Harry Wolfe who
     gave the first public lecture on child study in the

state of Nebraska (December 1892). He argued in favor of utilizing lay researchers. Such use of lay investigators became a key objection to the child study movement. Benjamin mentions that the movement's critics included William James, James Mark Baldwin, and Hugo Münsterberg, who wondered if child study was merely a popular fad.

66. Benjamin, Jr., L. (1987). A teacher is forever: The legacy of Harry Kirke Wolfe (1858-1918), *Teaching of Psychology*, 14, 68-74. Wolfe, described as a master teacher, not only was one of the first two Americans to earn a Ph.D. under Wundt but also was an early popularizer of the child study movement. During his long career at the University of Nebraska, he became a lecturer on child study, speaking to numerous teacher and parent groups throughout the region.

67. Buckley, K. (1989). *Mechanical man: John Broadus Watson and the beginnings of behaviorism*. New York: Guilford. This biography traces the career of the behavioral popularizer J. B. Watson. Following his scandalous divorce, Watson left academic psychology and entered advertising as an executive of the J. Walter Thompson Company. During the 1920's and 1930's, he became America's preeminent psychological expert through his prolific popular writings and radio broadcasts. His child care book, written with his second wife, was the most influential parental guide of its day.

68. Buckley, K. (1982). The selling of a psychologist: John Broadus Watson and the application of behavioral techniques to advertising, *Journal of the History of the Behavioral Sciences*, 18, 207-221. Watson pioneered efforts to apply scientifically derived principles of behavior to the advertising of products. Not only was he successful in using associationistic concepts in advertising strategy but also, through the expert testimonial technique, able to reinforce the notion that "experts" knew more than consumers about what was good for them. Buckley contends that Watson's message was strongly in support of an economic system that encouraged consumption for its own sake, and that, "Watson became the first 'pop' psychologist to the rapidly expanding middle class, assuming the role once held by the minister in a more rurally based society" (p. 217).

69. Cotkin, G. (1990). *William James, public philosopher.* Baltimore: Johns Hopkins University Press. This book describes both the private and the public William James. The champion of pragmatism, James, "delivered lectures to large crowds of 'great hulking rustics from prairie farms, with their thick hands' and to adoring Chautauqua visitors who celebrated American middle-class proprieties" (p. 12). His optimistic presentations offered an alternative message from the popular rantings of some of the Social Darwinists of the late nineteenth- and early twentieth-centuries.

70. Creelan, P. (1974). Watsonian behaviorism and the Calvinist conscience, *Journal of the History of the Behavioral Sciences*, 10, 95-118.

Speculative analysis of Watson's work as a reflection of his religious upbringing and his attempts to rebel against it. On the one hand, Watson, as an advertising executive, manipulated his fellow Americans to seek out various pleasures through buying and spending, while his child rearing advice is replete with "Puritan relics." Creelan refers to *Psychological Care of Infant and Child* as "a manual providing means of atonement for the new 'sins' of the parents" (p. 117).

71. Diamond, S. (1980). Francis Galton and American psychology, in R. W. Rieber and Kurt Salzinger (Eds.), *Psychology: Theoretical-historical perspectives*, (pp. 43-55). New York: Academic Press.

Galton, through his impact on Jastrow, Cattell, Woodworth, Terman, and Thorndike, greatly influenced the popularization of psychological notions. For example, Jastrow's exhibit at the 1893 World's Columbian Exposition in Chicago bore great resemblance to Galton's anthropometric laboratory.

72. Dinsmoor, J. (1992). Setting the record straight: The social views of B. F. Skinner, *American Psychologist*, 47, 1454-1463.

Describes several accounts in newspapers and popular magazines which unfairly label Skinner's views as totalitarian. The author argues that Skinner is more properly considered a libertarian than a totalitarian.

73. Duke, C., Fried, S., Pliley, W., and Walker, D. (1989). Contributions to the history of psychology: LIX. Rosalie Rayner Watson: The mother of a behaviorist's sons, *Psychological Reports*, 65, 163-169.

This paper describes a popular article written by Rayner Watson, the second wife and research collaborator of J. B. Watson. Surprisingly, Rayner Watson's popular piece, which appeared in *Parent's Magazine* in 1930, was somewhat negative regarding the use of behaviorism in the Watson home.

74. Evans, R. (1990). William James and his "Principles," in Michael Johnson and Tracy Henley (Eds.) *Reflections on "The Principles of Psychology" of William James after a century*, (pp. 11-31). Hillsdale, NJ: Lawrence Erlbaum Associates.

Writing of James's life prior to the publication of his *Principles*, Evans retells the story of the neurotic James clan. George Beard's article in 1869 popularized the notion of neurasthenia, and several members of the James family were living "proof" of the effects of the disorder.

75. Gay, P. (1988). *Freud: A life for our time.* New York: W. W. Norton.

This beautifully written volume places Freud in cultural context. Particularly relevant is a passage describing Freud as the premier popularizer of psychoanalysis for the better part of two decades, during which he condensed the *Interpretation of Dreams* into a briefer popular text, prepared encyclopedia entries, and even lectured to the B'nai B'rith.

76. Graebner, W. (1980). The unstable world of Benjamin Spock: Social engineering in a democratic culture, 1917-1950, *Journal of American History*, 67, 612-629.
Describes Spock as a member of an intellectual circle that included such luminaries as Erik Erikson, Kurt Lewin, Margaret Mead, and Elton Mayo. Asserts that Spock endeavored "to create a society that was more cooperative, more consensus-oriented, more group-conscious, and a society that was more knowable, more consistent, and more comforting" (p. 613). Contrary to critics who lambast the "permissive" nature of Spock's parental advice, Graebner contends that Spock's system viewed the competent parent "as a friendly boss." Many of Spock's principles are described in the context of progressive educational, developmental, psychological, and social-group-work theories of the 1920's, 1930's, and 1940's.

77. Hale, M. (1980). *Human science and social order: Hugo Münsterberg and the origins of applied psychology.* Philadelphia: Temple University Press.
Largely neglected in most histories of American psychology, Hugo Münsterberg relished the role of popularizer. An ardent German nationalist as well as Harvard professor, Münsterberg wrote books and articles on the traits of Americans, forensics, prohibition, psychotherapy, spiritualism, films, and a host of additional topics. Whether because of his

legendary abrasiveness, loyalty to Germany, penchant for self-promotion, or a combination of these factors, Münsterberg often found himself an object of ridicule by elements of the press and a number of his professional colleagues. His passionate defense of Germany during World War I raised suspicion of his being a spy, and his public attack on prohibition was viewed in some quarters as self-serving, since several of the key brewers of the day were German-Americans who had contributed funds to some of Münsterberg's various projects. Nonetheless, Matthew Hale makes a strong case for considering Münsterberg as "the 'founder' of applied psychology" (p. 188).

78. Hannush, M. (1987). John B. Watson remembered: An interview with James B. Watson, *Journal of the History of the Behavioral Sciences*, 23, 137-152.

The younger son of J. B. Watson and Rosalie Rayner Watson recalls, in rather painful fashion, the trials of being raised in strictly behavioristic fashion. James Watson believes that his father's views on sex "'created considerable trauma in my generation'" (p. 138). Though John B. Watson was the most prolific psychological popularizer of his time, his son remembers his father as actively avoiding public recognition.

79. Harris, B. (1984). "Give me a dozen healthy infants": John B. Watson's popular advice on childrearing, women, and the family, in Miriam Lewin (Ed.), *In the shadow of the past: Psychology portrays the sexes* (pp.

126-154). New York: Columbia University Press.
Watson's popular advice is examined in relation to the changing social context of the 1920's. During the period from 1926-1930, Watson wrote two books and over two dozen articles which concentrated on childrearing, women, and the family. The author contends that Watson's success as a popular expert was due in part to the dramatic changes in the female role in American culture. Watson engaged in a great deal of mother-bashing, blaming many of the problems of children on the inefficiencies of mother love.

80. Harris, B. (1979). Whatever happened to Little Albert? *American Psychologist*, 34, 151-160.
The author describes numerous flaws in the Watson-Rayner research with Little Albert and conditioned emotional response. Despite such flaws many textbook authors continue to consider this study to be definitive. Perhaps Watson's own popular writings contributed to this example of "myth making in the history of psychology" (p. 151).

81. Herrnstein, R. (1973). Introduction to John B. Watson's comparative psychology, In M. Henle, J. Jaynes, and J. Sullivan (Eds.), *Historical conceptions of psychology* (pp. 98-115). New York: Springer.
In an effort to spread the gospel of behaviorism, Watson published a series of popular articles and books during the 1920's. Typically the books were compilations of articles or popular lectures. Herrnstein describes the articles in

popular magazines as "interesting, forceful, and assertive, but they are also propagandistic, sometimes simplistic, and occasionally unscholarly. They seem to betray a mischievous pleasure in shocking their audience" (p. 111). Watson appeared to delight in questioning the morality of his day.

82. Joncich, G. (1968). *The sane positivist: A biography of Edward L. Thorndike.* Middletown, CT: Wesleyan University Press.

Contains several brief sections on popular science at the end of the nineteenth-century, James McKeen Cattell as popularizer, "The Human Nature Club, An Introduction to the Study of Mental Life" (a popular tome written for both Chautauqua groups and high school students), "Notes on Child Study" (written on a popular subject), as well as comments on Thorndike's prolific newspaper interviews, radio addresses, and public lectures. Scholars are aided by a detailed essay on sources and a highly detailed index.

83. Jones, L. (1980). *Great expectations: America and the baby boom generation.* New York: Coward, McCann, & Geoghegan.

Seeks to analyze the profound impact of the boomers on American culture. Of particular relevance is a chapter entitled, "From Spock to Sputnik," in which Dr. Spock is taken off the hook regarding charges that demand feeding of babies led to the coddling of American youth. Contrasts Spock's prescriptions for effective child rearing with the earlier advice of Emmett Holt and J. B.

Watson. Quotes Jackie Kennedy as proclaiming in 1960 that "Dr. Spock is for my husband, and I am for Dr. Spock" (p. 48). Spock himself was to become a highly visible political activist.

84. Kimble, G., Wertheimer, M., and White, C. (Eds.) (1991). *Portraits of pioneers in psychology.* Jointly published by Washington D.C.: American Psychological Association and Hillsdale, NJ: Lawrence Erlbaum Associates.

   Particularly relevant are chapters on William James, Joseph Jastrow, Ethel Puffer Howes, and John B. Watson. The popularizing of these four notables is described with the most detail given to Jastrow's efforts.

85. Kirschenbaum, H. (1991). Denigrating Carl Rogers: William Coulson's last crusade, *Journal of Counseling and Development, 69,* 411-415.

   The author criticizes William Coulson, a one-time associate of Rogers, who changed his views and found Roger's humanism wanting. Kirschenbaum details how Coulson utilized popular media, including television and radio talk shows, in an attempt to revise history by defining himself as one of the key figures in the development of humanistic psychology.

86. Kirschenbaum, H. (1979). *On becoming Carl Rogers.* New York: Delacorte Press.

   This biography offers an uncritical view of one of the most significant figures in the history of American psychology. The book includes a description of Rogers as a popularizer of encounter groups. Through tapes, films, and books, Rogers became the leading spokesperson for the group experience. By early 1978, his first trade book, entitled *Carl Rogers on Encounter Groups*, had sold around 240,000 copies. In order to promote the book, the publisher arranged for Rogers to make a guest appearance on the "Dick Cavett Show," but Rogers declined.

87. Minton, H. (1988). *Lewis Terman: Pioneer in psychological testing.* New York: New York University Press.
    A few sections of this biographical work are germane. Minton describes Terman's clearly anti-Semitic attacks upon Walter Lippmann of the *New Republic*. Later in this book, the author chronicles Terman's relationship with *The Reader's Digest* as well as his guest appearance on the "Quiz Kids" radio show. Terman hoped the latter activity would help to dispel various stereotypes of gifted children.

88. Modell, J. (1988). Meanings of love: Adoption literature and Dr. Spock, 1946-1985, In Carol Stearns and Peter Stearns (Eds.), *Emotion and social change: Toward a new psychohistory* (pp. 151-191). New York: Holmes & Meier.
    Insightful analysis of cultural meanings implied by popular texts on adoptive parenting as contrasted with Dr. Spock's views of the biological family. Spock's model is tied to a presumed physiological bond connecting mother to child. Modell describes changes in the adoption literature,

which reflect societal alterations in the ways in which not only adoption is viewed but in addition, modifications in cultural meanings given to parent-child relations in general. The author concludes, in this thoughtful and well-organized chapter, that present-day adoption manuals may communicate social meanings more reflective of American family life than the largely unchanged model promulgated by Benjamin Spock.

89. Moskowitz, M. (1977). Hugo Münsterberg: A study in the history of applied psychology, *American Psychologist*, 32, 824-842.

The author of twenty books and fifty-odd newspaper and magazine articles, Münsterberg was among the most prominent of psychology's popularizers since William James. Controversy frequently surrounded Münsterberg, who maintained a passionate German partisanship even though he resided in the United States for the last twenty-five years of his life until his death in 1916. This eclectic psychologist developed numerous applied interests in areas as diverse as psychotherapy, educational, industrial, and forensic psychology. According to Moskowitz, Münsterberg's lengthiest battle in the press involved mystical issues, and in this area, he stood firmly with those who rejected the paranormal. A series of his essays on legal applications was published in book form in *On the Witness Stand*, and Charles Klein shaped a play from material in the book. After the play was transformed into a film, Münsterberg became enamored with the film media and wrote a book on the subject. Prior to his death, he began work with Paramount Pictures as a scenario writer.

90. Ross, D. (1972). *G. Stanley Hall: The psychologist as prophet.* Chicago: University of Chicago Press.
This thorough and well-researched biography traces the life of an early popularizer of American psychology. Personal tragedies and a dogged commitment to the work ethic helped drive Hall to lead the applied child study movement and to contribute numerous articles on a wide variety of topics to popular magazines of his day.

91. Samelson, F. (1982). A note on an unpublished article by John B. Watson, *Journal of the History of the Behavioral Sciences*, 18, 20-21.
The author describes an unpublished article uncovered in the Watson collection in the Library of Congress. Entitled "The Modern Trend in Psychology," the set of galleys includes a note reading "Harpers Mag" and the document is stamped "REVISED."

92. Skinner, B. (1979). *The shaping of a behaviorist.* New York: Alfred A. Knopf.
The grand behaviorist recounts the tumult caused by his popular article on the air crib ("Baby in a Box", *Ladies' Home Journal*, 62 (October 1945), 30-31, 135-136, and 138). Skinner laments the problems caused by the title that the editors gave to the piece, that the photograph of his daughter, Debbie, showed her in the wrong crib,

and that the coverage given to the article by newspapers and radio stations was inaccurate.

93. Sokal, M. (1984). James McKeen Cattell and American psychology in the 1920's, in Josef Brozek (Ed.), *Explorations in the history of psychology in the United States* (pp. 273-323). Lewisburg, PA: Bucknell University Press.

Describes the 1920's as a period in which psychologists appeared to be extremely confident about their science and its numerous applications. This may have been due to an exaggeration of professional psychology's role in America's efforts during World War I. The popular press may have contributed to this overblown view of the profession's influence. Focus is placed on Cattell's career, the mental testing movement, industrial psychology, and child psychology.

94. Taylor, E. (1990). New light on the origin of William James's experimental psychology, In Michael Johnson and Tracy Henley (Eds.), *Reflections on "The Principles of Psychology" William James after a century* (pp. 33-61). Hillsdale, NJ: Lawrence Erlbaum Associates.

Includes mention of James's middle-brow writings in such organs as *The Nation* and *The Atlantic Monthly*.

95. Weiss, N. (1977). Mother, the invention of necessity: Dr. Benjamin Spock's *Baby and child care, American Quarterly*, 29, 519-546.

Contrasts Spock's work with the popular pamphlet, *Infant Care*, which was first published by the U.S. Department of Labor in 1914. A sample of the thousands of letters from mothers to the Labor Department's Children's Bureau from 1914 to 1928 are compared with letters sent to Dr. Spock. Letters written in response to *Infant Care* "revealed lives in vivid detail, including unwanted pregnancies, worry over ailing infants, brutal prairie living conditions, poverty, troubled husbands, and a medical profession largely indifferent to their needs" (p. 523). Unlike many bureaucratic organizations of the present day, Bureau members corresponded with letter writers, offering specific suggestions. Professor Weiss describes J. B. Watson's *Psychological Care of Infant and Child* as similar in its advice to *Infant Care* but very different in tone. With Watson, Mother is the problem, and Weiss contends that although Spock's techniques differ radically from Watson's, these two popularizers agree on one essential point: improper mothering can cause great harm. Letters to Spock are more literate than those sent in response to *Infant Care*. Many mothers offered high praise to Spock, but a few of the correspondents speak of grave matters like sexually abusing fathers, and the response sent is typically "get some counseling from a family social agency" (p. 535). Weiss suggests that the letters to Spock demonstrate how many mothers have internalized the values reflected by Spock's book. The advice is middle class in its world-view as was the case with the earlier *Infant Care*, but Weiss believes that working class mothers were able to accommodate the messages regarding social class in the Children's Bureau pamphlet.

96. Wiener, P. (1956). G.M. Beard and Freud on 'American nervousness,' *Journal of the History of Ideas*, 17, 269-274.

This rambling essay centers on Beard's "semi-popular" writings on American anxiety.

97. Zuckerman, M. (1975). Dr. Spock: The confidence man, in Charles Rosenberg (Ed.), *The family in history* (pp. 179-207). Philadelphia: University of Pennsylvania Press.

This chapter includes a critique of Spock's bestselling child rearing guide, which is described as "a manual of tension-management for parents, premised on a simple little confidence trick" (p. 184). Zuckerman asserts that Spock diverts his readers by instructing them to place trust in their own natural reactions. In somewhat contradictory fashion, Spock views the child as a truly "noble savage" and implores parents not to overdiscipline their children lest they be "products of parental ruination" (p. 187).

Psychoanalysis

This section of the research guide is devoted to the popularization of psychoanalysis in the United States. Soon after the 1909 lectures by Freud and Jung at Clark University, this school of thought began to take a foothold in popular circles. Citations cover the reception given to psychoanalysis in America, mass media interpretations, American popular psychology and religion movements which paved the way for analytic beliefs, the assimilation of psychoanalysis into American culture, popular attacks on psychoanalysis as well as analytic influences on child-rearing practices.

98. Burnham, J. (1979). From avant-garde to
     specialism: Psychoanalysis in America,
     *Journal of the History of the Behavioral
     Sciences*, 15, 128-134.

     According to Burnham, psychoanalysis
     began in America as an elite movement whose
     disciples included intellectuals and bohemians.
     Those who wanted to highlight the restrictive
     aspects of society often used psychoanalysis as a
     way to demonstrate hypocrisies of American
     society, and a number of individuals who were
     identified with the avant-garde took great pleasure
     in using concepts from psychoanalysis to shock
     and discount establishment figures. On occasion
     those who would disagree with their progressive
     notions were described as possessing motives with
     homosexual or incestuous elements. By the
     1930's, American psychoanalysts had developed
     close ties with so-called cultural elites who helped
     to spread its gospel to the larger American culture,
     and by the late 1940's, Burnham wrote: "The
     distinction between avant-garde and kitsch turned
     out to be a fine one indeed. In the process of all
     this vulgarization, psychoanalysis tended to lose its
     identity and to merge into a more general
     'psychologist mindedness'" (p. 132).

99. Burnham, J. (1988). The influence of psycho-
     analysis upon American culture, in John C.
     Burnham (Ed.), *Paths into American
     culture* (pp. 96-112), Philadelphia: Temple
     University Press. (Reprinted from Jacques
     M. Quen and Eric T. Carlson [Eds.]. 1978.
     *American psychoanalysis: Origins and
     development* (pp. 52-72). New York:

Brunner/Mazel, Inc.)

Describes the appearance of psychoanalysis in the mass media as inconspicuous during the 1930's, with sharp decline during the early years of World War II. By the late 1940's popularization was on the rise. Burnham writes that "By the 1960's, there were at least three children's books alone devoted entirely to Freud" (p. 103). Based upon citations in the *Reader's Guide*, there was an even greater interest after the Second World War in psychology in general than in psychoanalysis. Psychotherapists like Carl Rogers were described in popular offerings on equal footing with Sigmund Freud.

100. Demos, J. (1981). Oedipus and America: Historical perspectives on the reception of psychoanalysis in the United States, in Robert Brugger (Ed.), *Our selves/our past: Psychological approaches to American history* (pp. 292-306). Baltimore: The Johns Hopkins University Press.

Demos attempts to understand why psychoanalysis was so well accepted in many circles subsequent to Freud's 1909 American visit. By the mid-nineteenth century the family had been viewed as distinct from the rest of society. Psychoanalysis came in on the heels of a tradition of popular American child-rearing literature. The author writes that:

All authorities agreed on the extreme urgency of careful, responsible parenting. In speaking of parental responsibility Americans

actually meant maternal responsibility.
The goals of child-rearing, as expressed
in the advice literature, were somewhat
divided and confused. Discipline must
be based on appeals to conscience.
These different themes imply a massive
intensification of the parent-child bond
(pp. 298-299).

In addition to the advice literature leading the way
for Freudian thought, Demos argues that the
sentimentalization of the American mother as
glorified in popular culture vehicles like song may
have played into some Oedipal longings. Also
Demos suggests that immigrants, who flooded the
country, may have been cut off from the ties of the
European patriarchal family. While interesting
reading, the essay contains some broad leaps of
intellectual faith.

101. Evans, R., and Koelsch, W. (1985). Psychoanalysis
      arrives in America: The 1909 psychology
      conference at Clark University, *American
      Psychologist*, 40, 942-948.
      This famous meeting was well covered by
the local press. The conference organizer, G.
Stanley Hall, took great pains to assure positive
coverage by planting an anonymous article in *The
Nation*, a paper which he eventually included in his
list of publications. Apparently reporters from
Worcester and Springfield were provided English-
language abstracts of German lectures. The authors

suggest "that there was some prior arrangement assuring favorable coverage" (p. 947) in the *Boston Transcript* and that one needs to be cautious in concluding that such coverage suggests specific public interest or public opinion.

102. Gifford, G., Ed. (1978). *Psychoanalysis, psychotherapy and the New England medical scene, 1894-1944.* New York: Science History Publications/USA.

Chapters on "Boston at the Turn of the Century," William James, and G. Stanley Hall, an entire section entitled "Popular Psychotherapy Movements," which describes the activities of Mary Baker Eddy and the Emmanuel Movement, as well as a chapter by John Burnham on psychiatry in Boston of the 1920's make this book a valuable resource.

103. Green, M., and Rieber, R. (1980). The assimilation of psychoanalysis in America, in R. W. Rieber and Kurt Salzinger (Eds.), *Psychology: Theoretical-historical perspectives* (pp. 263-304). New York: Academic Press.

Chronicles the Americanization of psychoanalytic thought in American life. Discusses the role of the Emmanuel Movement and William James, popular magazine portrayals, and includes sections on popular books, art and movies, and politics and popular culture.

104. Hale, Jr., N. (1978). From Berggasse XIX to Central Park West: The Americanization of psychoanalysis, 1919-1940, *Journal of the*

History of the Behavioral Sciences, 14, 299-315.

In describing the path of psychoanalysis from Europe to the United States, the author emphasizes the role of American popular culture in shaping this form of psychotherapy. Writing in the late 1970's, Hale states that "the pervasive stamp of psychoanalysis is everywhere: middlebrow magazines, daily advice columns, and best-selling guides for parents" (p. 399). For example, there is a discussion of Karl Menninger's popularization of the death instinct in his book, *Man Against Himself.*

105. Hale, Jr., N. (1971). *Freud and the Americans: The beginnings of psychoanalysis in the United States, 1876-1917.* New York: Oxford University Press.

In a chapter entitled "Mind Cures and the Mystical Wave," the author describes the development of the Emmanuel Movement, which centered on religious psychotherapy. The movement's founder, Rev. Elwood Worcester, attempted to combine the powers of the self with psychotherapy and liberal Christianity. The author describes the role of popular magazine articles in stimulating the interest of such future psychoanalytic notables as A. A. Brill and Karl Menninger. General interest and family magazines of the period warned Americans about the possible emotional dangers of a fast-paced, success-oriented life. The author, in a chapter covering the popularization of psychoanalysis in the United States from 1909 to 1918, attributes its success to the following factors: the close relationship between American professional and popular culture, the widespread public fascination with mental healing, the young intellectuals who rallied around psychoanalysis, and the coverage in newspapers and magazines.

106. Hale, Jr., N. (1971). Introduction, in Nathan Hale, Jr. (Ed.), *James Jackson Putnam and psychoanalysis: Letters between Putnam and Sigmund Freud, Ernest Jones, William James, Sandor Ferenczi, and Morton Prince, 1877-1917*, (pp. 1-63). Cambridge: Harvard University Press.
Well written essay describing Putnam's place in the promotion of psychoanalytic thought in America.

107. Hornstein, G. (1992). The return of the repressed: Psychology's problematic relations with psychoanalysis, 1909-1960, *American Psychologist*, 47, 254-263.
Reports that American psychologists initially viewed psychoanalysis as another "mind cure" like Christian Science or the Emmanuel movement. After the famous Clark Conference of 1909, analysts began a campaign to win over the hearts and minds of the public. Most of the article serves as a description of psychology's response to psychoanalytic theory and concepts and to the profession of psychoanalysis.

108. Matthews, F. (1967). The Americanization of Sigmund Freud: Adaptations of psychoanalysis before 1917, *Journal of American Studies*, 1, 39-62.

Tracks the early responses to psychoanalysis from the intelligentsia of the day. Perhaps Freud helped to liberate them from "the ethic of self-restraint" (p. 50), that was a key aspect of the Puritanism that had been taught to many of the young intellectuals by their parents. Eventually, Freudian notions were utilized to help adjust the deviant to become "mature" by reflecting such behaviors as "productive action, responsibility to one's peers, smooth interpersonal relations" (p. 56). In other words, psychoanalysis started out in America as the domain of the intellectual radical and came to be incorporated as a mainstream tool of adjustment.

109. Morawski, J., and Hornstein, G. (1991). Quandary of the quacks: The struggle for expert knowledge in American psychology, 1890-1940, 106-133, in JoAnne Brown & David van Keuren (Eds.), *The estate of shared knowledge*. Baltimore: The Johns Hopkins University Press.

Traces two case studies in the popularization of psychology in America. The first case describes the response of psychologists to the rising popularity of psychoanalysis, while the second deals with the writings of Grace Adams, who was both a vehement critic of the popularization of psychology and a prolific popularizer in her own right. The authors view the boundaries between "expert knowledge," "common sense," and a "common science" as somewhat blurred and declare that: "Popularization is not a simple derivative or extension of scientific activity but rather entails transformation of knowledge"

(p. 126). As psychoanalysis became more and more popular, it proved to be a much larger problem for psychological science. Most significantly, since psychoanalysts were claiming dominion over matters of the mind, psychology could no longer assure its place as the discipline which controlled expertise over mental events. Early attacks against the analysts appeared in both scientific journals and the popular press, by such notable psychologists as Robert Woodworth and Christine Ladd Franklin. Another tactic chosen by experimentalists like E. G. Boring was to subject themselves to personal analysis and then to declare the process to be less than effective. A third response to psychoanalysis was to selectively choose concepts like reaction formation and study such notions scientifically while rejecting or ignoring the larger issues of the analytic perspective. In recent years, the American Psychological Association has been victorious in legal maneuverings over the American Psychoanalytic Association, with the former winning the right for its clinical constituents to gain access to psychoanalytic training. The second case outlined in this chapter describes the popularizations of Grace Adams from the late 1920's through the early 1940's. In earlier (1928-1934) writings, Adams criticized both psychologists and the general public. She attacked psychological theory, research, and popularization. After 1934, Adams' work, centered on common sense and the common wisdom of the public, included titles like *Don't Be Afraid* and *Your Child Is Normal*. The authors of this chapter conclude that the discipline of psychology has been less than successful in maintaining boundaries regarding expertise. Clearly, nonexperts continue to intrude on "disciplinary turf" (p. 127).

110. Steere, G. (1968). Freudianism and child-rearing in the twenties, *American Quarterly*, 20, 759-767.
Analyzes Freudian themes in popular parenting books published between 1925 and 1929. Steere checked for allusions to the following categories: sexual instincts, ego defense mechanisms, and the unconscious. Even though numerous scholars have described the influence of Freudian doctrine on the child-rearing of the 1920's, the author found little evidence of such in the forty-two manuals under scrutiny.

Behaviorism

In this section, the reader will find annotations covering historical references to behaviorism, the effects of behaviorism on the larger culture, and critiques of behavioral self-help approaches.

111. Birnbaum, L. (1955). Behaviorism in the 1920's,
      American Quarterly, 7, 15-30.
      Describes the acceptance of Watson's
      behavioristic principles, especially those regarding
      rigid child rearing. Birnbaum suggests that a
      generation of middle-class mothers were influenced
      by Watson's popular writings. Evidently, a
      booklet prepared by the Department of Labor
      entitled "Infant and Child Care" included all the
      major principles of Watson's program. As of
      1955, Birnbaum suggests that this booklet was read
      by a larger audience than any other publication of
      the federal government, and she reports that the
      contents of the manual had been only recently
      revised. According to the author, a return to
      conservative child rearing was occurring in the
      1950's.

112. Goldiamond, I. (1976).   Singling out self-
      administered   behavior   therapies   for
      professional   overview: A   comment   on
      Rosen, *American Psychologist*, 31, 142-147.
      The author argues that Rosen's proposal
      (found in the same issue of the *American
      Psychologist*) misses the mark and suggests that if
      the American Psychological Association were to
      enter the business of sanctioning various treatment
      techniques, deleterious consequences would surely
      follow. The author describes a television talk
      show featuring a behavior therapist who had co-
      authored a popular book on toilet training and
      another guest who represented a very different
      school of therapy. The latter guest displayed moral
      outrage, and an argument ensued with the host
      stepping in to defend the writer. Goldiamond

wonders how a therapist with a non-behavioral orientation could ever favor the widespread use of such a self-administered behavioral technique.

113. Lamal, P. (1989). The impact of behaviorism on our culture: Some e v i d e n c e a n d conjectures, *The Psychological Record*, 39, 529-535.

In a broad survey of behaviorism's possible impact on the larger culture, the author draws upon several popular sources. Much to the chagrin of the author, anecdotal evidence from an article appearing in a mainstream business magazine (*Fortune*) describes the application of "inner tennis" and wilderness survival to practical management concerns. The author also laments the noticeable absence of mention of books about behaviorism in such media outlets as *The New York Review of Books, Harper's, Atlantic Monthly,* and *The New Yorker* and appears to be pessimistic concerning the relative standing of behavior analysis in American culture.

114. Morris, E., Todd, J., Midgley, B., Schneider, S., and Johnson, L. (1990). The history of behavior analysis: Some historiography and a bibliography, *The Behavior Analyst*, 13, 131-158.

This quite useful article is comprised of an essay on historiography, a discussion of some key historical sources covering behavior analysis, and a selective bibliography. Any researcher pursuing work in the history of the application or popularization of classical or operant methods could benefit from consulting the bibliographical section.

115. O'Donnell, J. (1985). *The origins of behaviorism: American psychology, 1870-1920.* New York: New York University Press.

   As a social historian, O'Donnell views the gradual shift of American psychology from introspectionist to behavioristic from the bases of cultural, socioeconomic, and institutional pressures. After chronicling the contributions of such luminaries as Hall, Cattell, James, Yerkes, and Watson, the author of this text asserts that behaviorism and phrenology served similar interests in responding to progressive trends and the growing urbanization of America.

116. Rosen, G. (1976). The development and use of nonprescription behavior therapies, *American Psychologist*, 31, 139-141.

   In passing, Rosen compares current self-help programs with a popular book on personal magnetism published in 1913. Some of the more recent self-help tomes may have been validated empirically, but many were not. Suggestions are made for creating standards for self-administered behavioral interventions with the hope that if such standards are generated and followed, then effective programs may be purchased in local bookstores, which "may eliminate the need for many individuals to consult with professionals" (p. 140).

117. Todd, J., and Morris, E. (1992). Case histories in the great power of steady misrepresentation, *American Psychologist*, 47, 1441-1453.

Examines several areas in which behaviorism has been erroneously reported in both scientific and popular literature. Case examples include the role of environmentalism in both classical and operant behaviorism, totalitarian themes in behaviorism, and the alleged intellectual intolerance ascribed to behaviorists. These instances of academic folklore impede the development of psychology, and the authors provide a separate list of concrete recommendations for behaviorists and nonbehaviorists, so that such misrepresentations can be minimized. First on the list for behaviorists is the suggestion to write specifically for nonbehaviorist audiences.

Humanistic Psychology

This section covers criticism of some of the excesses of the popular elements of the humanistic movement. Excesses might include an overemphasis of the therapeutic benefits of strangers confronting strangers during a weekend encounter group, "open marriage", nude marathons, a "do your own thing" philosophy, and so forth. Social criticism of humanistic teachings and practice emanates from those on the political right, left, and center and often reflects concerns about the limitations of the liberalism of the 1960's and 1970's. Additional criticism comes from the psychological establishment. Annotations describe works devoted to political, social, and religious issues as well as more general historical treatments.

118.   Back, K. (1973). *Beyond words: The story of
       sensitivity training and the encounter
       movement* (2nd edition). New Brunswick,
       NJ: Transaction Books.
       Views sensitivity training and its related
       activities as a part of a larger social movement and
       describes the adherents of these endeavors as
       "pilgrims." In their quest to spread the joys and
       enlightenment often ascribed to some human
       potential experiences, many gurus, both lay and
       professional, took a clearly anti-intellectual posture
       in their defense of some of the movement's
       excesses.
       The second edition includes a new preface
       and a postscript. Suggests that the decline of
       sensitivity groups reflects dramatic changes in the
       larger culture and asserts that these groups "stress
       means over ends and the ambivalent relation to
       sensuality" (p. xvii).

119.   Back, K. (1974). Intervention techniques: Small
       groups. *Annual Review of Psychology*, 25,
       367-387.
       Views small group interventions of the
       1960's and 1970's as part of a social movement.
       Includes a brief history of the popularization of T-
       groups and encounter groups.

120.   Berger, A. (1990). *AGITPOP. Political culture
       and communication theory.* New
       Brunswick, NJ: Transaction Publishers.
       The term "agitpop" refers to "the political
       aspects of popular culture and the mass media" (p.
       xi). Of specific interest is a chapter on the human
       potential movement, centering on happenings in

Marin County, California. Uses an interview with George Leonard, a major human potential guru, to make points about the meanings and influence of this social movement. Highlights specific terms popular among humanistic practitioners.

121. Braginsky, B., and Braginsky, D. (1974). *Mainstream psychology: A critique.* New York: Holt, Rinehart and Winston. Provides a scathing attack of the psychologies of the late 1960's and early 1970's. The harshest criticism is levelled against the humanistic psychologists who are viewed as threatening human dignity through such superficial techniques as nude marathons. Maslow is portrayed as an elitist whose hierarchy of human motives is heavily slanted in favor of the upper classes.

122. Gendlin, E. (1987). A philosophical critique of the concept of narcissism: The significance of the awareness movement, in David Michael Levin (Ed.), *Pathologies of the modern self: Postmodern studies on narcissism, schizophrenia, and depression* (pp. 251-304). New York: New York University Press. Defends the "Awareness Movement" against those who would deem it to be narcissistic. An analysis of psychoanalytic criticisms of experiential psychology is presented in terms of the theories of Freud, Marcuse, and Kohut. Effort is made to clarify the concept of narcissism by differentiating ego strength and non-ego experience.

123. Haaken, J., and Adams, R. (1983). Pathology as "personal growth": A participant-observation study of Lifespring training. *Psychiatry, 46,* 270-280.

      The authors offer a critique of a popular form of human relations training of the 1970's and early 1980's. Psychologist Haaken and sociologist Adams utilize participant-observation from a psychoanalytic frame of reference. They argue that such "personal growth" training may encourage infantile helplessness, regression, and a pseudo self-awareness.

124. Johnson, B. (1981). A sociological perspective on the new religions, in Thomas Robbins and Dick Anthony (Eds.), *In gods we trust: New patterns of religious pluralism in America.* New Brunswick, NJ: Transaction Books.

      Comments on various aspects of the human potential movement in sections entitled "The Trend in Popular Religion" and "How the New Religions Differ from the New Therapies."

125. Koch, S. (1973). Psychology cannot be a coherent science, in Floyd Matson (Ed.), *Within/ Without: Behaviorism and humanism* (pp. 80-91). Monterey: Books/Cole.

      The author laments the lack of coherence in the science and practice of psychology in this essay, which originally appeared in a 1969 issue of *Psychology Today.* Psychology, unlike so many of its sister sciences, is not cumulative. In other words, each generation must rediscover certain psychological facts. In discussing the lack of coherence of the "depth" psychologies (e.g., humanistic), the author describes his experience in observing aspects of a pre-convention of humanists at an American Psychological Association meeting in the late 1960's. Koch's most direct hits concern the nude group therapy of Paul Bindrim and Maslow, whom Bindrim credits with the "insight" regarding the potential psychic release accompanying nudity.

126. Stone, D. (1981). Social consciousness in the human potential movement, in Thomas Robbins and Dick Anthony (Eds.), *In gods we trust: New patterns of religious pluralism in America* (pp. 215-227). New Brunswick, NJ: Transaction Books.

Based upon questionnaires and interviews, the author concludes that human potential participants appear more liberal and more active politically. Interestingly, Stone reports that among forty est graduates, "there is no clear trend toward political activism; there is a shift toward self-conscious involvement in family life, friendships, and for many, in more human potential trainings" (p. 222). Includes a discussion of some of the social outreach efforts of human potential groups like est's involvement with Project Hunger.

127. Wolfe, T. (1983). The me decade and the third great awakening, in Tom Wolfe, *The purple decades: A reader (pp. 265-293).* New York: Berkeley Books.

An earlier version of this essay first appeared in 1973. With acerbic wit, social commentator Wolfe lays waste to the excesses of the encounter group movement. In the opening lines of this piece, a sensitivity trainer encourages his flock to spew forth their repressed hang-ups, and heeding this therapeutic call, a young woman blurts out "Hemorrhoids." Encounter groups are labelled "lemon sessions," and "Lemon Session Central was the Esalen Institute. Esalen's specialty was a lube job for the personality" (p. 278).

Psychology and the Press

Under this heading, annotations cover historical cases of press coverage of psychological findings, the portrayal of psychology in the press, advice columns, the differing roles and responsibilities of journalists and psychologists in communicating psychology to a mass audience, and suggestions for both professions aimed at improving the quality of coverage of behavioral science.

128. Appley, D. (1987). Using *Psychology Today* articles to increase the perceived relevance of the introductory course, *Teaching of Psychology*, 14, 172-174.

    After having organized a list of the academic majors and career areas available at his institution, Appley assembled a bibliography of articles from *Psychology Today*. Two articles were selected for each of eighteen career fields.

129. Benjamin, Jr., L. (1988). Press coverage of psychology in the Rocky Mountains, *Journal of the History of the Behavioral Sciences*, 24, 98-101.

    The author describes local press coverage of clairvoyants and other pseudo-psychologists in the Denver area during the period from 1883-1927. In an effort to educate the public regarding the deceptive practices of mediums and palmists, Johns Hopkins professor Knight Dunlap journeyed to Fort Collins to deliver a series of public lectures, which were reported in the *Denver Post* on August 11, 1927. In addition, the author mentions how the local press virtually ignored meetings held during the first twenty-five years of the Rocky Mountain Psychological Association.

130. Benjamin, Jr., L., Rogers, A., and Rosenbaum, A. (1991). Coca-Cola, caffeine, and mental deficiency: Harry Hollingworth and the Chattanooga trial of 1911, *Journal of the History of the Behavioral Sciences*, 27, 42-55.

    Describes an early example of corporate-contracted psychological research. Discusses newspaper and magazine reactions to the trial in which Hollingworth's caffeine studies were highlighted. For example, from his position at *Good Housekeeping,* Harvey Wiley lambasted the Coca-Cola company for its use of caffeine.

131. Blake, R. (1948). Some quantitative aspects of *Time* magazine's presentation of psychology, *American Psychologist,* 3, 124-126 and 132.

Included is a content analysis of psychologically-oriented articles found in *Time* from January 1937, through June 1947. During this period, there were 271 psychological articles with nearly a fourth (61) concerning functional disorders. Blake compared the relative frequency of topics in *Time* with those appearing in *Psychological Abstracts* and found a similar set of frequencies under the various categories. The author suggests that while the *Time* articles are well-written, they do not include appropriate background and fail to provide the reader with a meaningful context.

132. Blakeslee, A. (1952). Psychology and the newspaper man, *American Psychologist,* 7, 91-94.

The author, a science reporter for the Associated Press, attempts to present a realistic view of newspapers for psychologists and emphasizes the speed with which stories are prepared. Admonishes psychologists that their stories must compete with all the other news. Blakeslee writes that "few stories in psychology are worth the investment of tremendous time and effort when there are as good or better stories to be had elsewhere" (p. 93). Blakeslee advises psychologists to limit their use of jargon when communicating with the press, because language is the greatest barrier for effective communication between psychology and the general public.

133. Dennis, P. (1989). "Johnny's a gentleman, but Jimmie's a Mug": Press coverage during the 1930's of Myrtle McGraw's study of Johnny and Jimmy Woods. *Journal of the History of the Behavioral Sciences*, 25, 356-370.

The author describes the popularization of McGraw's study of the Woods' twins and makes a case that the press played a role in the fall that psychology took in its public image. When the twin study began, popular literature on child rearing was growing in influence and held the promise of aiding in the alleviation of a myriad of social ills. McGraw's research was oversold to the public through newspapers and magazines, and, in addition, journalists shifted the focus from viewing McGraw's research from the effects of early training to a battle between heredity and behaviorism and, finally, to an examination of psychology's contribution to child rearing. The accompanying notes to Dennis' article provide numerous sources to the literature on the popularization of psychology.

134. Dibner, S. (1974). Newspaper advice columns as a mental health resource, *Community Health Journal*, 10, 147-155.

The author presents an analysis of one hundred letters received by two newspaper advice columnists, a male psychiatrist and a female psychologist. Of those requesting help, under thirty percent had previously sought professional help, over seventy five percent were written by women, and over thirty five percent requested general information about human behavior. There was a tendency for correspondents to blame others (e.g., spouse or child) for their difficulties. Dibner views the advice column as a resource through which "seeking advice may be a preliminary step in learning to identify one's problem and reformulate it vis-a-vis an appropriate and more professionally trained source. For others, writing to an advice columnist may be a last attempt to find help" (pp. 154-155).

135. Eron, L. (1986). The social responsibility of the scientist, In Jeffrey Goldstein (Ed.), *Reporting Science: The case of aggression* (pp. 11-20). Hillsdale, NJ: Lawrence Erlbaum Associates.

Reflects on personal experience when a *New York Times* reporter wrote a misleading story about the author's research findings. Argues that it is the researcher's responsibility to ensure that scientific findings are communicated accurately through the media.

136. Gaitz, C., & Scott, J. (1975). Analysis of letters to "Dear Abby" concerning old age, *The Gerontologist*, 15, 47-51.

Presents a content analysis of letters written by both older and younger persons regarding older adulthood. Two-thirds of the older correspondents were women as were three-fourths of the younger ones. Feelings of loneliness and rejection were expressed in the letters of the older writers, while younger writers communicated concerns about caring for their older family members. The legitimization of "Dear Abby" as an "expert" on gerontology is reinforced by *The Gerontologist* in the form of a one-half page addendum to the article, which was written by Abigail Van Buren ("Dear Abby").

137. Gerbner, G. (1961). Psychology, psychiatry and mental illness in the mass media: A study of trends, 1900-1959, *Mental Hygiene*, 45, 89-93.

Concludes that from 1900-1959 the relative number of magazine and newspaper articles devoted to psychological themes increased during times of war and prosperity and decreased during bad economic times.

138. Gerow, J. (Ed.) (1988). *Time: Psychology 1923-1986*. New York: Time, Inc.

This specially prepared issue of *Time* includes articles concerning psychology that appeared in the magazine from its inception in 1923 through 1986. Arranged chronologically, these pieces reflect media interest in psychological happenings from a report dated July 23, 1923 on Pavlov and classical conditioning to a 1986 piece on psychotherapy's effectiveness. Presented as a facsimile of a regular issue of *Time*, this periodical was designed as a companion to Gerow's general textbook, *Psychology: An introduction*, published in 1988 by Scott, Foresman and Company.

139. Gieber, W. (1960). The "lovelorn" columnist and her social role, *Journalism Quarterly*, 37, 499-514.

The author provides a content analysis of over five hundred letters written to an advice columnist over a span of several months. An effort was made to select every tenth letter, but the author does not state confidence in the sampling procedure. Almost ten percent were judged to be fakes, while another fifteen percent were labeled fan letters, offering praise or criticism to the columnist. Over seventy-five percent presented a problem with the largest category demonstrating a need for psychological counseling to treat a range of personal and interpersonal concerns. The author attempts to classify the tone of each letter by determining maturity, degree of tension, and perception of the problem. Also, the responses of the columnists are categorized by "action" suggested and by "tone." Interestingly, the columnist offered a "moral" response in over eighty percent of her answers. The author concludes the article by addressing the social functions of the columnist as both referee and "auditor to catharsis" and suggests several research hypotheses in need of examination.

140. Goldstein, J. (1986). Social science, journalism, and public policy, in J. Goldstein (Ed.), *Reporting science: The case of aggression* (pp. 1-10). Hillsdale, NJ: Lawrence Erlbaum Associates.

This is the first paper in a volume covering a meeting of violence researchers and science journalists. Goldstein ponders the "representativeness of science reporting and the representativeness of the reporting of violence research." Comments on the idea that article headlines and titles serve as editorials "as they present an interpretation of the reporter's article, which is, in itself, an interpretation of the scientist's research" (p. 4). Favors increased contact and cooperation between researchers and journalists so as to foster accuracy in reporting issues of social concern.

141. Jones, R. (1987). Psychology, history, and the press: The case of William McDougall and *The New York Times*. *American Psychologist*, 42, 931-940.

In an attempt to understand the role of the popular press in the declining reputation of McDougall, the author content analyzed articles appearing in *The New York Times* from 1906-1940. References to McDougall were contrasted with those concerning two of his peers, Joseph Jastrow and Edward Thorndike. There were significantly more emotionally laden headlines for articles on McDougall (e.g., "Forum on Behavior Most Misbehaved" and "Professor Duped in $22,800 Deal"). McDougall's positions were often misrepresented by headlines, and his positions were often satirized and ridiculed. The press may play a significant role in developing and maintaining the image of a psychologist and that individual's scientific positions.

142. LaFollette, M. (1990). *Making science our own: Public images of science, 1910-1955.* Chicago: University of Chicago Press.

Well-crafted analysis of the portrayal of science in popular American magazines. The general public was much more enamored of psychology's potential contributions to the greater good than was the case with the scientific community. The latter cast doubt on both the rigor of psychology's research methodologies and the measurability of concepts like emotion. Interestingly, as popular attacks on psychology multiplied during the 1920's and 1930's, the number of popular articles written by psychologists increased.

143. Lumby, M. (1976). Ann Landers advice column: 1958 and 1970, *Journalism Quarterly*, 53, 129-132.

Referring to Ann Landers' column as "short-order psychology," the author provides a comparison of the letters sent and the advice offered during the two years in question. Conclusions reached include a decrease from 1958 to 1970 in letters selected for the column that reflected the value of material goals, letters and advice that communicated increased tolerance regarding sexual variance, and a noticeable decrease in the frequency with which Landers suggested religious counseling. Lumby suggests that: "The enduring popularity of Landers' advice column suggests that she serves as a guide to the prevailing morality and provides a basis of common experience against which some readers--

particularly women--check moral judgments and behavior" (p. 132).

144. McCall, R. (1988). Science and the press: Like oil and water?, *American Psychologist*, 43, 87-94.
     The author concludes that press coverage given to the behavioral and social sciences is different from that given to the physical and biological sciences. In the case of the former:

> "The topics are more popular with editors and readers; researchers may be asked more frequently to generalize beyond the research to specific events or applications in society; commonplace terminology may be more easily misinterpreted; and such reports may compete with nonscientific sources of information on similar topics" (p. 92).

     Practical suggestions are given for improving relationships between journalists and scientists.

145. McCall, R., and Stocking, S. (1982). Between scientists and public: Communicating psychological research through the mass media, *American Psychologist*, 37, 985-995.
     The authors provide practical advice to psychologists on cooperating with the media, since they believe that if cooperation fails, then "the void is filled by nonscientists and pop psychologists" (p. 985). Mass media can be useful in influencing

behavior and social policy, so it behooves psychologists to learn how to interact more favorably with journalists. Included are helpful hints on how to be interviewed for newspapers, magazines, and television.

146. Miller, N. (1986). Appendix. A guide to effective communication with the media. In Jeffrey Goldstein (Ed.), *Reporting science: The case of aggression* (pp. 97-112). Hillsdale, NJ: Lawrence Erlbaum Associates.

Highly useful for scientists who wish to communicate accurately via popular media. Sections of this paper address controlling an interview, avoiding criticism from colleagues, giving credit to colleagues, preparing written statements, and judging reliability. Separate sections describe issues appropriate to television, radio, and newsprint.

147. Moran, J. (1989). Newspaper psychology: Advice and therapy, *Journal of Popular Culture, 22,* 119-127.

Describes a content analysis of six months of columns written by Joyce Brothers and Ann Landers in a local newspaper in 1986. Advice given seems to fit into "mainstream contemporary counseling psychology" (p. 125). However, both columnists demonstrated a tendency to agree with the correspondent's statement of the "facts," thus potentially alienating male readers. The author believes that since most of those seeking assistance were women, that men would be portrayed as the cause of most of the domestic problems. In addition, few referrals were made for professional help.

148.   Mott, F. (1957). *A history of American magazines, 1850-1865.* Volume II. Cambridge, MA: Harvard University Press.
       Especially relevant is material chronicling women's magazines.

149.   Mott, F. (1957). *A history of American magazines, 1 8 6 5 - 1 8 8 5 .* V o l u m e   I I I . Cambridge, MA: Harvard University Press.
       Readers are encouraged to review the chapter "Women and Their Magazines" as well as a section covering *Popular Science Monthly* whose inaugural issue included work by Herbert Spencer.

150.   Mott, F. (1957). *A history of American magazines, 1885-1905.* Volume IV. Cambridge, MA: Harvard University Press.
       The sections covering psychical phenomena, women's issues, and lyceum lectures are particularly useful.   A supplement includes sketches of such notable organs as *The Ladies Home Journal* and the *Woman's Home Companion*.

151.   Mott, F. (1968). *A history of American magazines: Sketches of 21 magazines 1905-1930.* Volume V.   Cambridge, MA: Harvard University Press.
       Relevant sketches cover *Better Homes and Gardens, Good Housekeeping,* and *Success. Success* was subtitled *A Magazine of Optimism, Self-Help, and Encouragement.*

152. Nelkin, D. (1987). *Selling science: How the press covers science and technology.* New York: W. H. Freeman and Company.
The author analyzes the role of journalists in shaping both public opinion and public policy regarding science. Relevant sections of the book cover psychosurgery and sociobiology. During the 1940's and early 1950's, psychosurgery was depicted favorably in the popular press and was viewed as an effective means of relieving pain and treating schizophrenia. By the 1970's, popular articles had a more negative tone and communicated more skepticism regarding the benefits of psychosurgery. The author believes that the changes in press coverage on psychosurgery may have reflected journalists' perceptions of changes in general social trends.

153. Powledge, T. (1986). What is "The Media" and why is it saying those terrible things about aggression research?, in Jeffrey Goldstein (Ed.), *Reporting science: The case of aggression* (pp. 83-89). Hillsdale, NJ: Lawrence Erlbaum Associates.
This science journalist suggests that scientists need to modify their behavior depending upon the particular media with which they are dealing. Argues that the relationship between scientists and journalists should remain adversarial.

154. Satariano, W. (1979). Immigration and the popularization of social science, 1920 to 1930, *Journal of the History of the Behavioral Sciences*, 15, 310-320.

In comparing popular articles by social scientists (including psychologists) with articles by representatives of the same professions in scholarly journals, the author finds popular articles more often were written in support of racist and discriminatory points of view. For example, articles appearing in popular organs were more likely to be written in favor of exclusionary quota laws. These popular essays provided the reading public with a somewhat skewed perspective on social scientific positions. Could it be that the editors of some popular magazines selected to publish those articles which supported their political agenda?

155. Schlossman, S. (1985). Perils of popularization: The founding of *Parents' Magazine*, in A. Smuts and J. Hagen (Eds.), *History and research in child development* (pp. 65-77). *Monographs of the Society for Research in Child Development*, 50 (4-5, Serial No. 211).

Description of the political maneuverings of George Hecht, an entrepreneur who came up with the idea for the popular magazine, Bearsley Ruml and Lawrence Frank, executives of the Laura Spelman Rockefeller Memorial Fund, who provided funding for the magazine, and Otis Caldwell and James Earl Russell of Teachers College, the institution through which the Rockefeller Fund subsidy was eventually funneled. Ever vigilant, the representatives were committed to defending "against vulgarization in the mass media, even if that required behind-the-scenes machinations, unorthodox corporate liaisons, and leaning on academic grantees." (p. 77).

156. Smith, T., and Levin, J. (1974). Social change in sex roles: An analysis of advice columns, *Journalism Quarterly*, 51, 525-527.

Advice columns from two time intervals, 1947-1951 and 1967-1971, are compared with regard to sex-role conceptions. Women comprised over 80% of the letter writers from both periods and the more recent advice more frequently takes the female's side against the male. The authors suggest that the advice column may be a unique barometer of society in that the column involves an interchange between the columnist and the audience.

157. Starker, S. (1989). *Evil influences: Crusades against the mass media*. New Brunswick, NJ: Transaction Publishers.

Fascinating historical account of societal overreaction to new forms of media. Describes how the guardians of American morality have led crusades warning of the evils of newspapers, novels, comics, movies, radio, television, rock videos, video games, and so forth. Each new medium of communication has been perceived as a threat to the public good by some political, religious, and scientific leaders. Starker provides numerous examples of how a myriad of social problems have been blamed on one particular form of media or another. It remains fashionable among the so-called intellectual elite to bash that which appears to be part of the "mass culture." Elitists

may argue that if something is popular, it cannot
be of truly high quality.

158.   Stocking, S. and Dunwoody, S. (1982). Social
       science in the mass media: Images and
       evidence, in Joan E. Sieber (Ed.). *The
       ethics of social research. Fieldwork,
       regulation, and publication* (pp. 151-169).
       New York: Springer-Verlag.
       Reviews evidence on the processes of mass
media, so that social scientists may make ethical
choices when disseminating research results. Cites
research documenting the lack of appropriate
training of many reporters covering social science
topics, summarizes research which emphasizes
various situational factors used to decide the
"newsworthiness" of a story, and data on the
accuracy of media stories and the role which
scientists may play in increasing the level of
accuracy. The authors include several ideas
regarding avenues of needed research and conclude
with a section covering practical implications.

159.   Tankard, J. and Adelson, R. (1982). Mental health
       and marital information in three newspaper
       advice columns, *Journalism Quarterly*, 59,
       592-597.
       The authors provide a content analysis of a
sample of the columns of Ann Landers, Abigail
Van Buren, and Joyce Brothers. Curiously, the
data demonstrate that Brothers, even though she
presented herself as a psychologist, tended to
support myths regarding mental health more than
Abigail Van Buren did but less than Ann Landers.

All three seem to be refuting such myths more than they are communicating accurate information regarding mental health.

160. Tavris, C. (1986). How to publicize science: a case study, in Jeffrey Goldstein (Ed.), *Reporting science: The case of aggression* (pp. 21-32). Hillsdale, NY: Lawrence Erlbaum Associates.

Describes anger over media response to the author's book on anger. Discusses the differing responsibilities of reporters and researchers. The latter demonstrate several language patterns (passive constructions, wordiness, and jargon) which contribute to errors in reporting. Advises researchers to utilize professionals to assist with publicity, editing, and so forth.

161. Valenstein, E. (1986). *Great and desperate cures: The rise and decline of psycho-surgery and other radical treatments for mental illness.* New York: Basic Books.

This well-written book chronicles the dismal behavior of scientists and practitioners in the development and application of the lobotomy and other forms of psychosurgery. The irresponsible and self-serving actions of a great many members of the medical community were given free rein by a popular press which failed to pass critical judgment. Articles, appearing in such mainstream organs of American journalism as *Reader's Digest, Harper's,* and the *Saturday Evening Post*, touted the wondrous miracle of the lobotomy while frequently underplaying possible risks. Clearly the proliferation of psychosurgical interventions was widened by a willing and amazingly uncritical press.

162. Viney, W., Michaels, T., and Ganong, A. (1980). An annotated bibliography of psychological articles in selected cultural magazines, abstracted in *Catalog of Selected Documents in Psychology*, 10, No. 3, 56, Ms. 2096 (The complete bibliography is available from Select Press). Annotations are provided for over 250 articles from *Atlantic Monthly, Forum, Harper's Magazine*, and *Popular Science Monthly*. Viney and associates include these four magazines since they are widely available, featured a number of articles of psychological content, and had appeal to a knowledgeable public. Organized in twenty content areas, entries include articles by Binet, James, Thorndike, and Watson.

163. Viney, W., Michaels, T., and Ganong, A. (1981). A note on the history of psychology in magazines, *Journal of the History of the Behavioral Sciences*, 17, 270-272.
A great many of the early eminent psychologists published articles in popular magazines. Such luminaries include Wundt, James, Hall, Münsterberg, and Watson. Although the authors suggest that popular articles may lack substance, carefully selected ones from general cultural magazines like *Harper's* or *Atlantic Monthly* may provide "a unique contribution to students' enjoyment of history" (p. 271). The authors utilize this note to describe their annotated bibliography (see Viney, Wayne; Michaels, Tom;

and Ganong, Alan, 1980). An annotated bibliography of psychological articles in selected cultural magazines, *Catalog of Selected Documents in Psychology*, 10, No. 3, 56, Ms. No. 2096.

164. Vokey, J., and Read, J. (1985). Subliminal messages: Between the devil and the media, *American Psychologist*, 40, 1231-1239.

The authors describe their research which shows a lack of evidence regarding effects of subliminal messages in advertising and popular music. They discuss the "treatment" that they and their research received in the media. When one of the authors agreed to be interviewed via the telephone for a radio program, he discovered that at the appointed time he was "live" on a call-in talk show. Although sloppy reporting in the media is noted, the authors point to what they consider to be the more fundamental problem of the media and the larger public, failing to appreciate the nuances of science and the scientific method.

165. Walum, L. (1975). Sociology and the mass media: Some major problems and modest proposals, *The American Sociologist*, 10, 28-32.

Describes the author's experience following media coverage of one of her academic papers. With continuing coverage of the paper in newspapers and on television, the "findings" of the paper changed. Walum likens the process to that of the development of a rumor and calls on the American Sociological Association to establish policies and procedures for scholars to deal with the public dissemination of their work.

166. Weigel, R., and Pappas, J. (1981). Social science and the press: A case study and its implications, *American Psychologist*, 36, 480-487.

    Provides a content analysis of press coverage regarding James Coleman's white-flight research. After examining over 200,000 pages of print media, the authors found that the white-flight hypothesis was reported in the popular press as scientific fact with very little critical analysis. The article concludes with several questions regarding the improvement of press coverage of social science, particularly psychological research.

167. Winsten, J. (1985). Science and the media: The boundaries of truth, *Health Affairs*, 4, 5-23.

    Describes the culpability of both the press and the research community in miscommunicating scientific findings to the public. One of the cases described in the article concerns Alzheimer's disease.

168. Wood, W., Jones, M., and Benjamin, Jr., L. (1986). Surveying psychology's public image, *American Psychologist*, 41, 947-953.

    The authors conducted a telephone survey of two hundred and one respondents in four major metropolitan areas. Over eighty-percent of those interviewed indicated that everyday living helps to provide training in psychological principles; over fifty-percent responded positively to an item regarding their likelihood to read about psychology from newspapers, magazines, and books; and about forty-percent mentioned that they had learned about psychology from television and films.

169. Yu, F. (Ed.) (1968). *Behavioral sciences and the mass media*. New York: Russell Sage.

   Presents papers from a 1966 conference for social scientists and journalists. Discusses dilemmas facing those who wish to communicate research findings to the lay public. Both journalists and scientists are portrayed as victims of their training and of the constraints of their contrasting professions. Among the strongest papers are those by Bogart, Bressler, Carter, Lippitt, and Ubell.

Self-help Books

Under this heading are citations on the following topics: the efficacy of popular psychology self-help books, ethical concerns, readability, self-help books from differing theoretical persuasions, commercialization, success and inspirational tomes, utilization of self-help books by health professionals, standards for evaluating and reviewing popular psychology books, narcissism and popular psychology books, and the history of self-help psychology books.

170. Barrera, M., Rosen, G., and Glasgow, R. (1981). Rights, risks, and responsibilities in the use of self-help psychotherapy, in Gerald Hannah, Walter Christian, and Hewitt Clark (Eds.), *Preservation of client rights: A handbook for practitioners providing therapeutic, educational, and rehabilitative services* (pp. 204-220). New York: The Free Press.
Spells out potential benefits as well as risks involved in self-help interventions. The consumer of these materials is faced with difficult choices. According to the authors: "Books on parenting, weight control, smoking cessation, and other multi-faceted problems often include a 'Chinese menu' of techniques that requires the reader to exercise judgment in making appropriate selections" (p. 211). Barrera and associates describe risks relating to improper assessment, the prescribing of treatment methods, and the possibility of failure. Included is a discussion of professional responsibilities as well as a section covering the following recommendations for action: (1) mental health professionals are advised to assist in the development of formalized standards for self-help materials; (2) professionals should communicate possible risks and benefits of these materials; and (3) they should become more actively involved in public education regarding self-help therapies.

171. Becvar, R. (1978). Self-help books: Some ethical questions, *Personnel and Guidance Journal*, 57, 160-162.
Thoughtful essay describing some ethical concerns including a tendency for books in this

genre to offer very liberal definitions of mental health and abnormality, which may have the effect of making everyone a prospective patient or client. Offers several "action suggestions." Challenges self-help authors to "fight pressures by publishers to hype a book and should insist upon advertisements whose limits are supported by research" (p. 161). But hype sells books!

172. Biggart, N. (1983). Rationality, meaning, and self-management: Success manuals, 1950-1980. *Social Problems*, 30, 298-311.

Analyzes thirty best-selling success books. Describes three images of success reflected in popular guides from 1750-1950: the Protestant ethic, the character ethic, and the personality ethic. Views these success tomes as fitting into four types: success-through-striving, entrepreneurial scheme books, manipulation manuals, and displacement books. Success-through-striving works, like *The Power of Positive Thinking*, center on the importance of the dream of success and stress cooperation and pleasantness as admirable behaviors. In the late 1950's and 1960's, entrepreneurial scheme books, such as *Anyone Can Make a Million*, became very popular. These works advise the reader as to how to make money (therefore, be successful) outside of a bureaucratic organization. Appearing in the 1960's through the 1980's are books which can be viewed as manipulation manuals. Works like *Body Language* and *Looking Out for Number One* counsel the reader on how to get ahead and "play the game" effectively. A fourth category, displacement books, instruct the reader on how to cope with life

outside the roles associated with work. Beginning
in the 1970's, books like *How To Be Your Own
Best Friend, The Relaxation Response*, and *Pulling
Your Own Strings* assisted the reader in dealing
with problems of self-esteem, stress, and self-
development. Biggart asserts that: "Underlying all
of these ideals of success has been a strong
middle-class belief in the meritocracy" (p. 306) and
concludes that these self-help books "encourage
workers to view themselves as objects and to
manage themselves in ways that hold no threat to
prevailing economic arrangements" (p. 298).

173.   Craighead, L., McNamara, K., and Horan, J.
       (1984). Perspectives on self-help and
       bibliotherapy: You are what you read, in S.
       Brown & R. Lent (Eds.), *Handbook of
       counseling psychology* (pp. 878-929). New
       York: John Wiley & Sons.
          Thorough review of empirical support for
       some self-help books. Calls for researchers to
       provide consumers with empirical evaluations of
       their programs. One of the more interesting
       aspects of the chapter is a preliminary delineation
       of assumptions which could characterize a model
       of self-help. The authors list six such assumptions,
       including the notions that, "techniques can be
       explained in simple language that can be under-
       stood by a lay person" and "persons are considered
       capable of self-initiating change" (pp. 882-883).
       Describes evaluations of self-help programs
       covering obesity, alcohol use, smoking, fear and
       anxiety, assertiveness, depression, sexual
       dysfunction, career indecision, and academic
       problems. Discusses three negative consequences

of some self-help programs: (1) lay persons may label themselves as emotionally disturbed or mentally ill when they are neither; (2) ineffective programs are available with most consumers not possessing the necessary information to make a solid judgment regarding their efficacy; and, (3) readers may misdiagnose themselves by selecting popular books addressing one problem, when their more significant "problem" may be something entirely different.

174. Davis, K. (1984). *Two-bit culture: The paper-backing of America.* Boston: Houghton Mifflin.
Traces the development of the American paperback book. The initial chapter includes an analysis of the success of Spock's *Baby and Child Care*, which Davis suggests as the second "most consequential paperback ever published" (p. 391 in the Appendix). Another self-help book, Dale Carnegie's *How to Win Friends and Influence People,* is the author's choice as the most influential. Suggests that the success of Carnegie's book was due to its providing Americans with a pep talk covering two significant needs: being successful in business and being liked by others. Views Carnegie "as the godfather of a long line of success purveyors" (p. 43) including Norman Vincent Peale and Wayne Dyer.

175. Dilley, J. (1978). Self-help literature: Don't knock it till you try it, *Personnel and Guidance Journal,* 56, 293-295.

Highly positive review of several popular books of the 1970's. Offers a few cautions including the idea that some persons who would be better served by individual counseling choose instead to follow the advice of a specific self-help guide.

176. Forest, J. (1987). Effects on self-actualization of paperbacks about psychological self-help, *Psychological Reports*, 60, 1243-1246.

Appropriate use of experimental research to determine the effects of reading a self-help book on a measure of self-actualization. Through the use of the Personal Orientation Inventory, this limited study lends support to the notion that popular self-help books may lead to a perception of greater self-actualization.

177. Glasgow, R., and Rosen, G. (1978). Behavioral bibliotherapy: A review of self-help behavior therapy manuals. *Psychological Bulletin*, 85, 1-23.

The authors provide a comprehensive review of over seventy-five self-help texts in the areas of assertiveness, child behavior, obesity, phobias, physical fitness, sexual dysfunctions, smoking, and study-skill building. Considered in this review article are written materials which reflect the behavioral approaches of aversive conditioning, desensitization, operant techniques, and modeling. Stresses the importance of experimentally validating such behavioral self-help programs.

178. 	Henderson, B. (1983). Self-help books emphasizing transpersonal psychology: Are they ethical?, *The Journal of Transpersonal Psychology*, 15, 169-171.
	This brief essay addresses concerns regarding lack of adherence to the American Psychological Association's Code of Ethics among some authors who write popular self-help books of a humanistic bent. Admonishes writers of these texts to focus more on just what they hope to achieve, on any explicit or implicit claims, and on the specific audience being addressed.

179. 	Kimbrell, G. (1975). Note: Diet dilettantism, *The Psychological Record*, 25, 273-274.
	Castigates authors and publishers of popular diet books which promise the reader success. Views these books as "too food oriented." Suggests that behavior modification programs constructed on an individualized basis offer the best hope for real change for the obese person.

180. 	ʼMullins, L., and Kopelman, R. (1984). The best seller as an indicator of societal narcissism: Is there a trend? *Public Opinion Quarterly*, 48, 720-730.
	Fascinating study which endeavors to quantify the presence of narcissism in American society as reflected by best-selling books. Through content analysis, the researchers counted books which centered on such topics as self-improvement and personal growth and found an increase in the proportion of narcissistic texts from 1950 to 1979. Perhaps, a weakness of this effort is the authors'

equating narcissism with self-improvement and personal growth. Apparently Mullins and Kopelman have operationalized a definition of narcissism reflecting popular instead of clinical terms; in other words, they appear to have used a pop definition of narcissism as the basis for this empirical work. Nevertheless, it is a clever and valuable bit of research.

181. O'Farrell, T., and Keuthen, N. (1983). Readability of behavior therapy self-help manuals, *Behavior Therapy*, 14, 449-454.

Following a recommendation from the American Psychological Association's Task Force on Self-Help Therapies concerning the reading level of self-help materials, the authors provide an evaluation of the readability of 124 behavioral manuals. Suggest that much of the available self-help material may be at a reading level beyond the ability of a significant number of American adults.

182. Ogles, B., Craig, D., and Lambert, M. (1991). Comparison of self-help books for coping with loss: Expectations and attributions, *Journal of Counseling Psychology*, 38, 387-393.

Flawed but interesting evaluation of four self-help books on adjustment to the breakup of a marriage or other relationships. Volunteers were divided into four experimental groups, with subjects in each group given a different self-help guide. Subjects were administered pre- and post-test instruments with the result being that all four groups of subjects indicated equally positive results with all of the books, which may be significant since the four texts were written from different perspectives and presented in differing formats. This preliminary study suggests the need for a great deal more evaluative research on the efficacy of self-help materials.

183. Riordan, R., and Wilson, L. (1989). Bibliotherapy: Does it work?, *Journal of Counseling and Development*, 67, 506-508.

Briefly reviews studies which approach the subject of the effectiveness of various forms of bibliotherapy. Offers three conclusions: (1) there is a steadily growing number of behaviorally oriented materials that have been validated empirically (at least on a minimal level); (2) materials of a fictional or inspirational nature are less likely to be scientifically evaluated; and (3) there appears to be increasing interest in the use of bibliotherapy among counseling practitioners.

184. Rosen, G. (1981). Guidelines for the review of do-it-yourself treatment books, *Contemporary Psychology*, 26, 189-191.

The author provides a set of seven guidelines for reviewers of self-help books. Rosen is appalled at the number of such books written by psychologists that describe untested programs, use misleading titles, and spout exaggerated claims. He hopes that high quality reviews of self-help books will help encourage a higher degree of professionalism on the part of the authors of these mass market offerings.

185. Rosen, G. (1987). Self-help treatment books and
     the commercialization of psychotherapy,
     American Psychologist, 42, 46-51.
          Cautions psychologists who publish self-
     help materials. Self-administered treatments have
     been shown to be much less successfully applied
     than those administered by a professional therapist,
     and problems can even worsen as a result of
     unsuccessful self-help interventions. Psychologists
     are admonished to guard against exaggerated
     claims made by the publishers of their self-help
     products. Recommends that the American
     Psychological Association circulate sample
     materials that psychologists could use as a frame of
     reference in dealing with their publishers over
     misleading claims in titles or book jackets. Earlier,
     Rosen had chaired the American Psychological
     Assocation Task Force on Self-help Therapies
     (1978) which issued a report.

186. Rosen, G. (1978). Suggestions for an editorial
     policy on the review of self-help treatment
     books, *Behavior Therapy*, 9, 972.
          Abstract of an extended report which
     admonishes book reviewers to rely more on data-
     based evaluations of self-help books. Critical of
     reviewers who fail to include judgments
     concerning the clinical efficacy of programs
     offered in popular books.

187. Saper, Z., and Forest, J. (1987). Personality
     variables and interest in self-help books,
     Psychological Reports, 60, 563-566.
          Reports on an experimental study of 122
     college students. Found a relationship between

neuroticism as measured by the Eysenck Personality Inventory and interest in self-help materials. The authors cast doubt on the reliability of their own data. This research is preliminary at best.

188. Schneider, L., and Dornbusch, S. (1958). *Popular religion: Inspirational books in America.* Chicago: University of Chicago Press.

    Content analytic study of American popular religious writings. Religious bestsellers were chosen for study if the books were within the Judeo-Christian tradition, offered "techniques," and addressed "everyday problems of everyday people." Includes a listing of thirty-five themes characteristic of this genre. According to the authors, psychological themes emerge in this literature in the 1930's and continue to be important. In a chapter entitled, "Psychotherapy, Magic, and Mass Culture," religious tomes are placed in the larger context of mass culture.

189. Starker, S. (1988). Do-it-yourself therapy: The prescription of self-help books by psychologists, *Psychotherapy*, 25, 142-146.

    Reports on a mail-questionnaire study of 121 psychologists. Almost seventy percent of those who returned the survey indicated that some of their clients described a perception of being helped through self-help books. Most of the psychologists who were queried believe that such popular materials are sometimes or often helpful, and over sixty percent of the therapists mentioned that they prescribe such books, with books on parenting being the ones most frequently prescribed.

190. Starker, S. (1989). *Oracle at the supermarket: The American preoccupation with self-help books.* New Brunswick, NJ: Transaction Publishers.
      Historical treatment of the place of the self-help book in American life. Exceptionally well-documented, this book should be consulted by all who are interested in the development of popular psychology. Traces the emergence of pop books from the works of colonial New England clergy through the fulfillment texts of the 1980's. Every chapter is strong but particularly valuable are the ones titled, "Classical Self-Help: The Early Blockbusters," detailing the works of Rabbi Joshua Liebman, Dale Carnegie, Arnold Gesell, and Benjamin Spock and chapters on the 1980's and "prescriptions and promises" for the future. In the last two chapters, Starker includes tentative conclusions, which in themselves could generate a number of important research questions, including: (1) Are the benefits of popular texts merely due to a placebo effect or do some of these books offer useful information and strategies for successful life changes? (2) Are consumers concerned with the scientific validation of the materials which they purchase? (3) What values are communicated by the self-help books?

191. Starker, S. (1986). Promises and prescriptions: Self-help books in mental health and medicine, *American Journal of Health Promotion*, 1, 19-24, 68.
      This article describes two survey studies conducted in the Pacific Northwest. Potential

consumer respondents were selected out of the telephone book for the first study, with almost sixty-five percent of them having read a very helpful self-help book. When rating such books in general, over eighty percent viewed such works as "sometimes helpful" or "often helpful." In a companion study, Starker mailed questionnaires to psychologists, psychiatrists, and internists whose names appeared in the Portland and Seattle phone books. Almost half of the psychologists believed their clients utilized self-help books very often or often. Almost ninety percent of the psychologists prescribed popular works, as did almost sixty percent of the psychiatrists and eighty-five percent of the internists. Starker suggests that these findings help to document the notion that "the self-help book has quietly established a niche in the practice of psychology, psychiatry, and internal medicine" (p. 24).

Radio and Television Psychology

This section is devoted to the uses of media psychology for community education, the possible advantages and disadvantages of serving as a radio or television psychologist, positive and negative experiences of some who have served in such capacities, recommendations for media psychologists, content analyses of broadcast media, public evaluation of the content and effectiveness of radio psychology programming, as well as historical treatments of radio psychology.

192. Bouhoutsos, J., Goodchilds, J., and Huddy, L. (1986). Media psychology: An empirical study of radio call-in psychology programs, *Professional Psychology: Research and Practice*, 17, 408-414.

   The introduction to this paper includes a history of radio psychology programs. The first such programs were offered by the Popenoe Institute of Family Relations in Los Angeles in the 1950's. KABC initiated syndication of several call-in programs, including one hosted by psychologist, Toni Grant. This article reports findings from two studies, one a survey of 368 shopping mall patrons and the other a telephone survey of 122 callers to a New York-based radio program. Almost half of the respondents in the former study had listened to a radio call-in psychology program, and the advice given to the callers who were respondents in the latter study was deemed by most of them to be helpful. The authors conclude that the data suggest that "these hosts present a positive image of psychologists to the public, at least to that public that listens to and calls such programs" (p. 414).

193. Dain, N. (1989). Critics and dissenters: Reflections on "anti-psychiatry" in the United States, *Journal of the History of the Behavioral Sciences*, 25, 3-25.

   This paper outlines efforts to bash American psychiatry. Criticism has come from several sources: ex-patients, social scientists, and political reformers. In 1987, critics took to the airwaves in New York City and promoted their views via a monthly program called "The Madness Network."

Since anti-psychiatric sentiments come from a number of groups, the movement has been splintered. As a recognition of the movement's strength, ex-patients were invited to the 1985 meeting of the American Psychiatric Association. The author believes that the anti-psychiatry movement is in disarray. The messages of voluntarism and the plethora of self-help groups may reflect an anti-psychiatry mentality, points which Dain neglects to mention.

194. Harris, L., and Hamburg, M. (1990). Back to the future: Television and family health-care management, in Jennings Bryant (Ed.), *Television and the American family* (pp. 329-347). Hillsdale, NJ: Lawrence Erlbaum Associates.

Includes a description of seventeenth-through early twentieth-century popular guides to medical self-care. Discusses the growth of the knowledge base in health care and argues that television as a source of health information is greatly lacking. Areas of concern include such topics as alcohol, violence, and sexual practices. Sees the potential of interactive video for family health-care education.

195. Klonoff, E. (1983). A star is born: Psychologists and the media, *Professional Psychology: Research and Practice*, 14, 847-854.

Views psychologists as potentially effective consumer educators and social commentators. Mass media interventions can offer treatment to those who might not seek it through more traditional avenues and can aid in the prevention of future psychological dysfunction and in the "demystification" of psychology. The public can be harmed if media psychologists present inaccurate, simplistic, or unrealistic information and guidance. Perhaps, some psychologists utilize the media to build their private practices or to become known as "experts" or "stars." The success of media psychology may be due in large part to the public's seemingly "insatiable curiousity about psychological matters" (p. 851).

196. Levin, M. (1987). *Talk radio and the American dream*. Lexington, MA: D.C. Heath.
According to political scientist Levin, the rise of talk radio reflects a corresponding rise in working-class alienation. Levin pontificates on the meaning of this growing form of mass media. This is an important book for those interested in radio psychology.

197. Levy, D., Emerson, E., and Brief, D. (1991). Radio psychology talk show hosts: Assessment of counseling style, *Journal of Community Psychology*, 19, 178-188.
Analyzes the styles of a sample of radio psychologists. Using a fourteen-category system for analyzing counseling style, these researchers report that the hosts' styles reflect the directive and active approaches of Albert Ellis and Fritz Perls, although hosts appeared less confrontational than Perls and more supportive and disclosing than Ellis. In explaining the results of this study, Levy and colleagues suggest that on-air style is largely due to the time limitations of a radio program and the needs of the larger audience for information.

198. Levy-Leboyer, C. (1988). Success and failure in applying psychology, *American Psychologist*, 43, 779-785.

The author voices concerns about the many misapplications of psychological findings. Citing his own research on psychology and the environment, he describes his experience as a guest on a radio broadcast during which he was asked to offer professional pronouncements on topics ranging from the best color to paint a baby's room to the ideal size of a classroom. The broadcast organizer was disappointed by the author's approach to answering the various questions by pointing out the unique aspects of each situation. As a vivid example of the readiness to communicate and apply psychological findings, the author notes the wide acceptance of Maslow's hierarchy of needs despite a total lack of empirical evidence in its support.

190. Liebert, R., and Sprafkin, J. (1988). *The early window: Effects of television on children and youth* (3rd edition). New York: Pergamon Press.

Comprehensive review of relationships between television viewing and the behavior of children. Replete with references to both academic sources and popular articles written by both behavioral scientists and lay persons.

200. McCall, R., Gregory, T., and Murray, J. (1984). Communicating developmental research results to the general public through

television, *Developmental Psychology*, 20, 45-54.

A series of twenty news features under the title, "The 'Science for Families' Project," was created by a team of developmental psychologists and producers, with an estimated viewing audience for any single episode between 12.4 and 29.1 million people. McCall and associates suggest that developmental psychologists and television producers can be effective collaborators. Advice is offered for psychologists who may be potential sources for news or who may appear as guests on television or radio talk shows. Would-be talk show guests are admonished to be prepared, to avoid jargon and any tendency to ramble, and to try to control the interview by providing the interviewer, prior to the interview, with a summary of the psychologist's book or article and a listing of credentials, title, and areas of expertise.

201. Monaghan, J., Wah, A., Stewart, I., and Smith. L. (1978). The role of talkback radio: A study, *Journal of Community Psychology*, 6, 351-356.

Views talkback radio as an important vehicle for crisis intervention. This empirical study was constructed to assess the role of such radio programming as a source of help-giving. Community members did not view talkback radio as a significant source of help-giving. Apparently, entertainment was the more important need served.

202. Saxe, L. (1991). Lying: Thoughts of an applied social psychologist, *American Psychologist*, 46, 409-415.

Saxe describes his participation in the design and implementation of an investigation/demonstration of four polygraph examiners for "60 Minutes." Millions of television viewers witnessed this experimental deception. Using CBS's and his use of deception to debunk polygraphers, Saxe describes a possible role for psychology in understanding the phenomenon of lying.

203. Schwebel, A. (1982). Radio psychologists: A community psychology/psycho-educational model, *Journal of Community Psychology*, 10, 181-184.

As host of a radio call-in program in Columbus, Ohio, the author experimented with a variety of psycho-educational techniques (e.g., brag nights in which callers were asked to call and "stroke" themselves, mini-lectures, question and answer sessions on specific topics, and so forth). These radio practices are guided by a set of six postulates: (1) people are their own best health resource; (2) many persons have difficulty in discussing personal problems; (3) people may lack training in problem solving; (4) solutions to some problems may be within one's control, while solutions to other problems may be outside the individual; (5) most people can find greater joy in life; and (6) positive thinking can be very helpful. Suggests that radio psychologists view themselves as community psychologists first and as broadcasters second.

204. Taylor, W. (1957). Gauging the mental health content of the mass media, *Journalism Quarterly*, 34, 191-201.

A method for counting and categorizing mental health themes in mass media is presented. Proportionately more such messages were recorded via broadcast media than by magazines, with newspapers lagging behind magazines. Those persons described as abnormal were shown as looking and acting in different ways than the so-called normal. Other frequent messages include: everyday stressors can drive one crazy; there are relationships between physical problems and psychopathology; and therapists, particularly psychiatrists, are upright and intelligent.

Psychological Testing

Under this heading are annotations on the popular response to psychology's role in testing soldiers during World War I, discussion by such defenders of psychology as Robert Yerkes, Lewis Terman, and Henry Goddard as well as the criticism of Walter Lippmann regarding testing, immigration, and purported racial distinctions, Thomas Alva Edison's amateurish attempts at test construction and administration, the popularized debate between Richard Herrnstein and critics like Leon Kamin over IQ and "meritocracy," the misrepresentation of expert opinion on testing in the popular press, and more general historical presentations.

205. Aby, S. (1990). *The IQ debate: A selective guide to the literature.* Westport, CT: Greenwood Press.

Included are annotations for 408 sources on the controversies surrounding IQ. The author has selected English-language works and has arranged the book in two parts, with the first covering relevant bibliographies, indexes, abstracts, databases, handbooks, dictionaries, and encyclopedias, and the second portion including books, book chapters, professional journal articles, magazine articles, newspaper articles, ERIC documents, and media materials. The sections covering magazine and newspaper articles describes fifty-seven and forty-one popular citations respectively.

206. Brown, J. (1991). Mental measurements and the rhetorical force of numbers, in JoAnne Brown and David van Keuren (Eds.), *The estate of social knowledge* (pp. 134-152). Baltimore: The Johns Hopkins University Press.

Argues that during the Progressive Era professional psychologists utilized language associated with engineering and medicine in efforts to bolster disciplinary prestige and sell the public on psychology's claim to expertise in mental testing. Includes a discussion of the criticism and defense of testing, which appeared in the popular press in the early 1920's.

207. Chapman, P. (1988). *Schools as sorters: Lewis Terman, applied psychology, and the intelligence testing movement, 1890-1930.*

New York: New York University Press.
Includes a chapter entitled "Rising Dissent: Controversies over Intelligence Testing," which describes Walter Lippmann's scathing attacks in the *New Republic*.

208. Cravens, H. (1978). *The triumph of evolution: American scientists and the heredity-environment controversy, 1900-1941.* Philadelphia: University of Pennsylvania Press.
Engaging historical treatment describing the hereditarian bent of many American social scientists. Strong chapter on mental testing which includes a discussion of Walter Lippmann's popular assault on those social scientists who espoused the elitist and racist Nordic hypothesis regarding immigrants and intelligence. Particularly relevant is a description in the concluding chapter in which Cravens states that "by the 1940's, scientists of man, could now present to educated Americans a unified, coherent, evolutionary science. The processes of popularization were complex indeed. Certainly the new ideas were disseminated in college lecture halls, in the newspapers, magazines, over the radio and television" (pp. 271-272). Cravens views the developing role of the behavioral science professor as including the educating of a new group of experts in human relations (both semi-professional and professional) on such diverse topics as personnel management, family relationships, the assessment of intelligence, and most recently, "the narcissism of contemporary self-help psychology" (p. 272).

209. Cravens, H. (1985). The wandering IQ: American culture and mental testing, *Human Development*, 28, 113-130.

The article begins with a description of a report which appeared in the November 7, 1938, issue of *Time* magazine. The *Time* article reported on the controversial findings of psychologists at the Univerity of Iowa's Child Welfare station concerning the malleability of intelligence. Although such reasoning was considered heretical by some, the author argues that it should be understood in terms of changes in the larger American culture. As a cultural historian, the author makes a case that science is culture bound.

210. Cronbach, L. (1975). Five decades of public controversy over mental testing, *American Psychologist*, 30, 1-14.

Magazines geared toward the educated public, particularly *The New Republic, Atlantic Monthly,* and the *New York Times Magazine,* have played a significant role in disseminating controversial opinions regarding testing, social class, and race. Many scientific arguments appear to have been greatly misrepresented in these popular magazines, and Cronbach believes that "Journalism has no corrective for misstatements that are popular" (p. 11). Academics are cautioned to consider the possible public reactions to socially relevant research and to consider this in making written statements for public media which might be misconstrued or sensationalized by eager journalists.

211. Dennis, P. (1984). The Edison questionnaire, *Journal of the History of the Behavioral Sciences*, 20, 23-37.

Thomas Edison developed a "test" in 1921 which purported to measure an individual's knowledge of general information. Edison made some incredible claims regarding his "instrument," such as that his testing of college graduates showed they were "amazingly ignorant." The test received widespread coverage in the popular press which may have contributed to the development of a number of very inadequately constructed personnel tests and, moreover, may have played a role in the loss of status of the mental test in American society.

212. Fancher, R. (1985). *The intelligence men: Makers of the IQ controversy*. New York: Norton.

Examines the modern debate over intelligence and its relationship to nature and nurture. Particularly pertinent is the description of the vicious attack on Richard Herrnstein after his summary article appeared in a 1971 issue of the *Atlantic Monthly*. Although his article did receive some thoughtful criticism and support, a number of his detractors, who seemingly misunderstood his paper, labeled him a racist and threatened him with violence, which caused among other things the cancellation of a Herrnstein lecture on animal psychology scheduled to be delivered at Princeton.

213. Herrnstein, R. (1973). *I.Q. in the meritocracy*. Boston: Little, Brown, and Company.

Outgrowth of the author's famous (infamous) popular article, which appeared in the

Atlantic Monthly (September 1971, pp. 43-64). Attempts to make an argument in support of the notion that "social standing (which reflects earnings and prestige) will be based to some extent on inherited differences among people" (pp. 197-198).

214. Kamin, L. (1974). *The science and politics of I.Q.* Potomac, MD: Lawrence Erlbaum Associates.
Scathing critique of the heritability argument for intelligence and of the politicization of psychology in furthering that point of view. Takes numerous swipes at such popularizers as Herrnstein and Jensen.

215. Pastore, N. (1978). The Army intelligence tests and Walter Lippmann. *Journal of the History of the Behavioral Sciences*, 14, 316-327.
In the early 1920's a debate raged between well-known psychometricians, notably Lewis Terman and Henry Goddard, and their critics exemplified by Walter Lippmann. This debate emerged from publicity surrounding the *Army Report*, which asserted the average mental age of white draftees to be 13.08 years, and that approximately 47.3 percent of the general population might qualify as morons. In biting attacks in the *New Republic* and *Century Magazine*, Lippmann accused several psychologists of "yellow science."

216. Samelson, F. (1979). Putting psychology on the map: Ideology and intelligence testing, in

Allan Buss (Ed.), *Psychology in social context* (pp. 103-168). NY: Irvington Publishers.

Includes a discussion of the public debate over intelligence and immigration which occurred during the 1920's in American newspapers and in such magazines as *The New Republic* and *Atlantic Monthly.* Samelson suggests that among the popularizers from psychology were scholars like Lewis Terman and Robert Yerkes who viewed themselves as liberal-progressives, even though their arguments are often seen as quite racist by today's standards.

217. Samelson, F. (1977). World War I intelligence testing and the development of psychology, *Journal of the History of the Behavioral Sciences*, 13, 274-282.

Documents public reaction to the significant role played by a number of psychologists in World War I. Samelson cites the work of Hornell Hart who statistically analyzed popular magazines during the period from 1900 to 1930. Working under the auspices of Hoover's Commission on Social Trends, Hart demonstrated that there was very little interest in psychological topics during the first decade of the century, but by the early 1920's, such articles appeared more often than any other of the sciences with the exception of what were termed commerical applications (movies, radio, and automobiles). The present author describes how professional psychology encouraged publicity surrounding its involvement in the war.

218. Snyderman, M., and Rothman, S. (1987). Survey of expert opinion on intelligence and aptitude testing, *American Psychologist*, 42, 137-144.

Even though there is great controversy in the larger culture regarding intelligence testing, a survey of experts shows positive attitudes regarding both the utility and validity of intelligence and aptitude tests. A great number of stories appearing in the popular media do not reflect this level of support for testing among experts.

219. Snyderman, M., and Rothman, S. (1990). *The IQ controversy: The media and public policy.* New Brunswick, NJ: Transaction Books.

Using a content analysis of media presentations and a survey of experts on intelligence, the authors provide an analysis of media coverage surrounding contrasting views on testing for intelligence, aptitude, and achievement. The media have not accurately presented the views of psychometric experts, and Snyderman and Rothman contend that "fairness and accuracy are not the norm in news media coverage of intelligence and aptitude testing" (pp. 247-248). Extreme positions on the genetic/environment debate have been given much airtime and space in print, which has contributed to the dramatic differences between public and expert opinion.

220. Sokal, M. (1987). Introduction: Psychological testing and historical scholarship: Questions, contrasts, and context, in Michael Sokal (Ed.), *Psychological testing and American Society: 1890-1930*, (pp. 1-

20). New Brunswick, NJ: Rutgers University Press.

Beginning the essay with a discussion of the ongoing debate over the role of standardized testing in American society, Sokal describes several popularizations and misrepresentations of psychometric findings. The author briefly describes the eighteenth- and nineteenth-century practice of using physiognomy (reading one's temperament and character from the face) and discussed its heir to popularity, phrenology. Sokal contends that phrenology, through mental exams and "professional" advice, functioned in its day much as consulting psychology has in the twentieth century.

221. Wachhorst, W. (1981). *Thomas Alva Edison: An American myth.* Cambridge: MIT Press.

Includes a discussion of the quizzes that Edison developed in 1921 and 1922. Few of the college-educated job applicants who took these "tests" passed them, which Edison took as a symptom of the failure of the American educational system. The press seemed to enjoy the controversy that was generated. Edison's assault on the failure of higher education hit a populist chord because Edison was a symbol of the American themes of hard work and practical application, and he was a hero who could do just about anything, including develop intelligence tests.

Children, Romance, and the Family

Several interwoven topics from the history of popular psychology are cited in this section of the research guide. Specifically, these annotations address analysis of popular prescriptions for parenting, nonparental care, love relationships, family dynamics, and divorce.

222. Anderson, H. (1990). The congregation as a healing resource, In Don Browning, Thomas Jobe, and Ian Evison (Eds.), *Religious and ethical factors in psychiatric practice* (pp. 264-286). Chicago: Nelson-Hall.

Viewing the religious community as a highly appropriate vehicle for preventive mental health, Anderson describes several education and training courses available at churches and synagogues. Included are educational offerings geared to parents of adolescents, single parents, and children of divorce.

223. Arluke, A., Levin, J., and Suchwalko, J. (1984). Sexuality and romance in advice books for the elderly, *The Gerontologist*, 24, 415-419.

Through content analysis compares advice books published before and after 1970. The findings of the study offer some support for the general improvement in American society of attitudes toward older adult sexuality. More recent advice books tend to encourage elders to maintain their levels of activity in many spheres of life, but these same popular works continue to be somewhat negative on the issues of dating and remarriage for elderly persons.

224. Bane, M. (1973). A review of child care books, *Harvard Educational Review*, 43, 667-680.

Review essay which includes general comments on the functions of popular child care books. Describes a number of bestselling books and pamphlets, which were published between 1959 and 1973. Asserts that such guides are typically tailored to the raising of the first child because young parents are most anxious and uncertain about the specifics of child care. Suggests that popular books relieve anxiety by supplying useful information.

225. Bernal, M., and North, J. (1978). A survey of parent training manuals, *Journal of Applied Behavior Analysis,* 11, 533-544.

Provides a thorough examination of twenty-six popular parenting manuals. Each parent training guide is analyzed by the following categories: the specific audience targeted, reading level, presence of technical language, glossary, whether or not it is based on programmed learning, availability of supplementary material, a listing of published reviews, and the type of research evaluation used if any. Contains a comprehensive table which includes all the pertinent characteristics of the texts under consideration.

226. Bloom, L. (1976). "It's all for your own good": Parent-child relationships in popular American child rearing literature, 1820-1970, *Journal of Popular Culture,* 10, 191-198.

Spotlights representative child rearing texts of a 150-year period. These books are viewed as idealistic and as hierarchical with God or a psychotherapist as superior, followed by a parental adviser, the parent, and lastly, the child.

227. Brieland, D. (1957). Use of research in recent popular parent education literature, *Marriage and Family Living,* 19, 60-65.

In analyzing current parent education literature (mostly from 1955 and 1956), the author finds infrequent citation of research findings. In an effort to understand the underlying reasons for this finding, several possible explanations are offered. Among these explanations are: (1) a number of problems studied by researchers may not be interesting to parents, (2) researchers may write specifically for their peers, and (3) statistical terms may serve as a barrier in presenting research findings to parents.

228. Bruch, H. (1954). Parent education or the illusion of omnipotence. *American Journal of Orthopsychiatry*, 24, 723-732.
Describes several mistakes common in parent education. So-called "family experts" may undermine parental authority and may, in fact, practice a form of hypocrisy. On the one hand, parents and teachers are told to be considerate or even permissive regarding the child, but this same message is communicated by a "stern and authoritarian tone. It often sounds like talking down to blank-faced automatons who are just made to put into practice the experts' pet theory about 'what is best for the child'" (p. 730).

229. Butler, J. (1976). The toilet training success of parents after reading *Toilet Training in Less Than a Day*, *Behavior Therapy*, 7, 185-191.
Parents were instructed on how to toilet train their children through three weekly classes, the use of Azrin and Foxx's self-help book, *Toilet Training in Less Than a Day*, written instructions, and telephone calls. Over three-fourths of the parents were

successful in their toilet training efforts within a two-month period. Since there was no direct observation of actual parental methods, this study does not serve as an evaluation of Azrin and Foxx's procedure.

230. Clark, H., Greene, B., Macrae, M., Patrick, M., Davis, J., and Risley, T. (1977). A parent advice package for family shopping trips, *Journal of Applied Behavioral Analysis*, 10, 605-624.

Describes the experimental development of a popular package for parents. Demonstrates that empirical procedure can be used to design practical materials for dissemination to the public.

231. Clarke-Stewart, K. (1978). Popular primers for parents. *American Psychologist*, 33, 359-369.

In response to a questionnaire, the vast majority (ninety-four percent) of a random sample of Chicago parents indicated they had read at least one popular article or book on the care of children. Although reaction to the popular works was generally positive, there were frequent criticisms that the guides were impractical, lacked specificity, and were too permissive. Clarke-Stewart advises authors of popular child care material to be responsive to the needs of their audience.

232. Contratto, S. (1984). Mother: Social sculptor and trustee of the faith, in Miriam Lewin (Ed.), *In the shadow of the past: Psychology portrays the sexes. A social and intellectual history* (pp. 226-255). New

York: Columbia University Press.
Describes several psychological
pronouncements on mothering which were made
from the end of the nineteenth-century through the
1970's. Includes discussion of G. Stanley Hall's
participation in the National Congress of Mothers,
J. B. Watson, applications of psychoanalysis in
popular parenting literature, the National Congress
of Parent Education, Arnold Gesell and cognitive-
developmental theory as well as American and
British trends occurring after 1940. The author
concludes with comments on why certain notions
of mothering continue, asserting that psychologists
have assumed the role of guides to parenting,
which was performed previously by clergy who
occupied that cultural position in the nineteenth-
century. The model of "Mother as social sculptor"
offered sanctuary in a world exploding with change
and gave men a scientifically sanctioned excuse for
failing to participate fully in the caring and
socialization of their young.

233. Etaugh, C. (1980). Effects of nonmaternal care on
       children. Research evidence and popular
       views, *American Psychologist*, 35, 309-319.
       Includes a general analysis of popular books
and articles published from 1956-1976 on the
subject of nonmaternal care of children. Using
books and articles from five high circulation
"women's magazines," Etaugh categorized the
message as negative, positive, or mixed. By the
1970's popular writings were reflecting a much
more positive view of nonmaternal care. Such
popular pundits as Brazelton continued to warn
against the dangers of such care, while Benjamin

Spock, by the 1976 edition of his *Baby and Child Care*, changed his position somewhat, although he did proclaim "that the best caretakers in the first 3 years are parents" (p. 315 in Etaugh). Negative views persist in some of the popular literature, even though scientific writings are much more positive. Etaugh reasons that some of this difference may be due to the larger publication lag with books compared with articles in popular magazines.

234. Geboy, M. (1981). Who is listening to the "experts"? The use of child care materials by parents, *Family Relations*, 30, 205-210.
     This study involved mail surveys and telephone interviews in Tyler, Texas, an East Texas community of approximately 70,000 residents. Almost ninety-seven percent of the parents had read child care materials when their children were young. The author conjectures that one factor that might encourage the use of such information by parents "may be the implication in the titles of many child care manuals that parents need assistance in rearing their children" (p. 209).

235. Hillman, C. (1954). An advice column's challenge for family-life education, *Marriage and Family Living*, 16, 51-54.
     After analyzing over 6,400 letters written from women to the author of a popular magazine advice column, Hillman concludes that there has been a societal failure to instruct people in the ways of appropriate personal and family life. The correspondents sought assistance on many matters

including premarital sex, infidelity, alcoholism, and sexual incompatibility.

236. Kelly, R. (1974). *Mother was a lady: Self and society in selected American children's periodicals, 1865-1890.* Westport, CT: Greenwood Press.
Analyzes both explicit and implicit social messages reflected in the youth magazines of the era. Kelly includes discussion of contemporaneous commentary of social scientists like G. Stanley Hall and concludes with a useful bibliographical essay.

237. Kidd, V. (1975). Happily ever after and other relationship styles: Advice on interpersonal relations in popular magazines, 1951-1973, *Quarterly Journal of Speech,* 61, 31-39.
This speculative study views popular magazines as contributing to a shared symbolic vision of the real world. While analyzing themes regarding interpersonal relations, the author identifies two different visions of social reality. In the first, behavior is labelled as wrong or right, condemned or acclaimed. In the second vision, which began sometime in the 1960's, relationships are perceived as ever changing with the meaning of any interaction being negotiable.

238. Lewis, J. (1989). Mother's love: The construction of an emotion in nineteenth-century America, in Andrew Barnes and Peter Stearns (Eds.), *Social history and issues in human consciousness: Some interdiscipli-*

nary connections (pp. 209-229). New York: New York University Press.
By the 1830's, popular magazines like the *American Ladies' Magazine* and *The Mother's Magazine* were defining women as the prime socializers of their children. Mother's affection was supposed to balance father's rationality.

239. Lomax, E., Kagan, J., and Rosenkrantz, B. (1978). *Science and patterns of child care.* San Francisco: W. H. Freeman.
Describes and analyzes relationships between scientific views of child rearing with more popularized points of view. Lucid sections cover nineteenth-century parental advice literature, Arnold Gesell, Freud's influence on parental practice, and trends in advice on infant care, 1900-1940.

240. Matthews, F. (1988). The utopia of human relations: The conflict-free f a m i l y i n American social thought, 1930-1960, *Journal of the History of the Behavioral Sciences,* 24, 343-362.
Rambling essay which attempts to cover the image of the family in popular writings against the background of thirty years of American social history. Concedes that popular social engineers like Watson and Spock promoted their positions, but the author asserts that the public was ready for the message. Argues that by the 1930's, readers of expert advice received ideas reflecting a "perceived crisis of the family" (p. 347), ideas that were central to the work of such social scientists as Harold Laswell in his *Psychopathology and*

Politics and by John Dollard and his associates in their seminal work, *Frustration and Aggression*. Matthews suggests that "by the mid-1940's, the doctrine that the family was key to social problems... had become conventional wisdom among the helping professions" (p. 350). Benjamin Spock offered parents a paradox: they must trust their own inclinations but in so doing not frustrate their children. Above all, parents were encouraged to relax with their children. But Spock was not overly concerned with the frustrations of mothers because he so strongly prescribed that mothers not work outside the home. At certain points in his writings, Spock allows that some professional women seek employment; to do otherwise would make them unhappy. But if these mothers were to choose a career, then they would not be attending to their responsibilities as mothers. The essay concludes with the generalization that "The universal brotherhood of mankind would be realized through scientific child-rearing, so as to produce a community of open, tolerant personalities... Deweyite progressives and emigre socialists shared the utopian inheritance of the Enlightenment, the belief in the universal kingdom of harmony realized through scientific human engineering" (p. 358).

241.   Mechling, J. (1975). Advice to historians on advice to mothers, *Journal of Social History*, vol. 9, 44-63.

Objection is made to the use of child-rearing manuals in historical research. The context of advice may greatly differ because of time and place. There may be a sampling bias, in that certain classes may be more likely to be aware of child-rearing advice. The author asserts "that child rearing manuals are the consequence not of child rearing values but of child rearing manual-writing values" (p. 53).

242. Morawski, J. (1984). Not quite new worlds: Psychologists' conceptions of the ideal family in the twenties, in Miriam Lewin (Ed.), *In the shadow of the past: Psychology portrays the sexes* (pp. 97-125). New York: Columbia University Press.

The author describes and analyzes the utopian visions of G. Stanley Hall (Atlantis), William McDougall (Eugenia), and J. B. Watson. In addition, there is a discussion of some humorous treatments of psychology that appeared in newspapers and popular magazines. Perhaps, these humorous yet derisive commentaries reflected public concern over the unfulfilled promise of psychology to make the world a better place.

243. Nance, R., (1970). G. Stanley Hall and John B. Watson as child psychologists, *Journal of the History of the Behavioral Sciences*, 6, 303-316.

A number of references are made to efforts at popularization made by both Hall and Watson. Hall is described as one who "made frequent speeches in his role as interpreter of the new genetic psychology" (p. 306), and six of Watson's popular articles which appeared in *Harper's Magazine* from 1926-1928 are cited. Nance's paper seems to ramble and comes to no clear conclusions.

244. O'Neill, W. (1967). *Divorce in the Progressive Era.* New Haven, CT: Yale University Press.

Drawing on popular writings, O'Neill analyzes conservative and liberal positions regarding divorce in America during the period from 1890-1920. Includes a bibliography of popular books and pamphlets.

245. Pollock, L. (1985). *Forgotten children: Parent-child relations from 1500 to 1900.* Cambridge: Cambridge University Press.

Argues that it is inappropriate "to infer parenting behavior from advice in manuals" (p. 46). This comment and other relevant thoughts can be found in the second chapter, which serves as a criticism of the literature on the history of the treatment of children.

246. Ryerson, A. (1961). Medical advice on child rearing, 1550-1900, *Harvard Educational Review*, 31, 302-323.

Views the medical advice literature along the lines of oral, anal, sex, dependence, and aggression training. The advice changed regarding giving a newborn a purge, feeding by schedules, using wet-nurses, recommended age for weaning, use of cradles, teething as a dangerous disease, magical cures for teething, use of cold baths for children, swaddling, sex-play among children, masturbation, independence for children, and whether the child had been born good or evil.

247. Shields, S., and Koster, B. (1989). Emotional stereotyping of parents in child rearing manuals, 1915-1980, *Social Psychology Quarterly*, 52, 44-55.

Through an examination of fifty-four child rearing guides from six discontinuous eras between 1915 and 1980, the authors find that mothers are depicted as overly emotional, while fathers are viewed as more objective in response to their children. A frequent warning from popular manuals reflects the dire consequences that may befall a child if the mother is overly emotional.

248. Skolnick, A. (1991). *Embattled paradise: The American family in an age of uncertainty.* New York: Basic Books.

Utilizes commentary from popular as well as scholarly sources in viewing the changes in American family life. Argues that all is neither awful nor wonderful in the contemporary family. A useful bibliography contains a good mix of historical, psychological, and sociological material.

249. Slater, P. (1976). *The pursuit of loneliness: American culture at the breaking point* (Revised edition). Boston: Beacon Press.

This book provides thoughtful social criticism. Especially useful is the discussion of child rearing and the impact of Spock on the beliefs and practices of American parents. Slater contends that Spock reinforced traditional views regarding women's roles and encouraged the guilt of mothers and their overinvolvement in the lives of their children.

250. Stewart, A., Winter, D., and Jones, A. (1975). Coding categories for the study of child-rearing from historical sources, *Journal of Interdisciplinary History*, 5, 687-701.

The authors spell out the need for an objective coding system for analyzing the content of child-rearing manuals from the past. They offer the following general categories: nursing, child-rearer, family structure, sex-differentiation of children, dependence/independence training, admired virtues in children, vices condemned in children, style of punishment, attitudes toward learning, and attitudes toward "manners." Included as appendixes to the article are the complete coding system and a comparison with three previous studies.

251. Sunley, R. (1955). Early nineteenth-century American child-rearing literature, in Margaret Mead and Martha Wolfenstein (Eds.), *Childhood in contemporary cultures* (pp. 150-167). Chicago: The University of Chicago Press.

Summarizes themes reflected in popular child-rearing literature from 1820 to 1860. Emphasis was placed on the primacy of the mother to the virtual exclusion of the father, gradual weaning, dangers associated with overfeeding and drugging of infants, issues associated with motor development and independence, toilet training, sexual behavior including masturbation, and moral development. Throughout much of this period, mothers were to insist upon total obedience and submission of their children, and indulgence was perceived as particularly harmful. At least three schools of thought regarding the nature of the child emerged: a Calvinist view which assumed depravity, a "hardening" one related to the writings of Locke, and a "gentle treatment" approach.

252. Vincent, C. (1951). Trends in infant care ideas, *Child Development*, 22, 199-209.

This article contains a review of infant care as recommended by women's magazines during the period from 1890-1948. Magazine articles from the 1890's emphasized a loose scheduling for infants, by the 1920's mothers were being advised to tightly schedule their offspring, and by 1948 mothers were encouraged to self-regulate according to the baby's particular needs. The author believes that child-care writers have reflected emerging middle-class values in their prescriptions rather than a cogent body of knowledge.

253. Wishy, B. (1968). *The child and the republic: The dawn of American child nurture.* Philadelphia: University of Pennsylvania Press.

Traces popular advice on child-rearing in the years from 1830 to 1900. A body of popular literature on the subject emerged by the 1830's. Wishy cites John Hall's 1836 complaint concerning "the current of popular treatises on this subject that almost daily issues from the press" (p. 4). In the latter part of the nineteenth-century, Darwinian notions grew to have a greater and greater impact on child rearing tracts. By the turn of the century, parents were instructed to make every effort to raise happy as well as obedient children. An extensive bibliography contains a thorough listing of both primary and secondary sources.

254. Wolfenstein, M. (1954). Fun morality: An analysis
      of recent American child-training literature,
      in Margaret Mead and Martha Wolfenstein
      (Eds.), *Childhood in contemporary cultures*
      (pp. 168-178). Chicago: The University of
      Chicago Press.

      The author analyzes the content of the
      Infant Care bulletin of the Children's Bureau, a
      Department of Labor publication. In contrasting
      earlier editions (1914-1921) with more recent ones
      (1942 and 1945), Wolfenstein finds significant
      change in the advice given to parents. In earlier
      editions, infants are depicted as bundles of
      impulses whose penchant for masturbation and
      thumb-sucking must be eliminated, and mothers are
      told not to play with their offspring. On the other
      hand, mothers are encouraged to display
      nonchalance in response to the baby's
      autostimulation and to facilitate healthy exploratory
      play in the more recent bulletins.

255. Wolfenstein, M. (1953). Trends in infant care,
      American Journal of Orthopsychiatry, 23,
      120-130.

      Analyzes seven editions of *Infant Care*, a
      popular child-care bulletin issued by the U.S.
      Children's Bureau. Viewing versions of the
      manual published between 1914 and 1951,
      Wolfenstein chronicles shifts in advice regarding
      masturbation, thumb-sucking, breast feeding, and
      bowel and bladder training. Writing from a
      psychodynamic point of view, the author assumes
      that even though the parental advice encourages
      more and more maternal tolerance, many moms
      continue to be uncomfortable about some of baby's

physical activities, although these same mothers may repress such feelings.

256. Wrigley, J. (1989). Do young children need intellectual stimulation? Experts' advice to parents, 1900-1985, *History of Education Quarterly*, 29, 41-75.

This paper describes the content analysis of over a thousand articles from about sixty different popular magazines. From the first decade of the century to the eighth, articles concerning intellectual stimulation of the very young increased dramatically. To illustrate the haphazard nature of some "expert" advice, the author describes several articles from early in the century which attest to the potential harm to babies through such stimulation.

257. Young, K. (1990). American conceptions of infant development from 1955-1984: What the experts are telling parents, *Child Development*, 61, 17-28.

Content analysis of thirty years of the two popular publications. During this time period, *Parent Magazine* published 443 articles on infants. Based upon the topical categories used in the study, forty-seven percent of these articles contained information reflecting theory and research from the discipline of child development, while fifty-three percent of the articles offered information on practical or medical aspects of infant care. The thematic content analysis supports the notion that research has strongly influenced expert advice to parents, especially in the areas of cognition, perception, and temperament. In topical areas such as the mother-infant relationship, feeding, and child care, advice appears to be more related to broad demographic and cultural changes.

258. Young, K. (1991). What parents and experts think about infants, in Frank Kessel, Marc Bornstein, and Arnold Sameroff (Eds.), *Contemporary constructions of the child: Essays in honor of William Kessen* (pp. 79-90). Hillsdale, NJ: Lawrence Erlbaum Associates.

This essay includes a section entitled "A History of Expert Advice about Infant Development."

Popular Psychology and Women

Selections in this chapter reflect feminist themes. Citations center on scholarly commentary in regards to popular psychological messages to women, especially in the areas of sexuality, male-female relationships, dieting, career success, and "female maladies." Many of the references discuss the mixed messages provided to women by so-called "psychological experts" and the effect of women purchasing the majority of self-help books, a fact not lost on publishers and authors.

259. Altman, M. (1984). Everything they always wanted you to know: The ideology of popular sex literature, in Carol Vance (Ed.), *Pleasure and danger: Exploring female sexuality* (pp. 115-130). Boston: Routledge & Kegan Paul.
    Provides a feminist analysis of such works as *Everything You Always Wanted to Know about Sex (But Were Afraid to Ask)*, Masters and Johnson's *The Pleasure Bond, The Joy of Sex, The Sensuous Woman, The Sensuous Man, Any Woman Can*, and other sexual advice books of the late sixties and early seventies. Twenty years ago, these works appeared to be quite radical and liberating but in retrospect can be viewed as conservative, sexist, and stereotypic. These guides included much information on physiology and sexual practice which was often misleading and at times clearly incorrect.

260. Bate, B., and Self, L. (1983). The rhetoric of career success books for women, *Journal of Communication*, 33, 149-165.
    Analyzes seventeen success books published between 1975 and 1981. The authors were interested in understanding how the concept of success was delineated, how the relationship between the author and the reading audience was developed in each text, and how authors portrayed women. Bate and Self find a lack of agreement among the authors of success books about just what comprises success.

261. Brownell, K. (1991). Dieting and the search for the perfect body: Where physiology and

culture collide, *Behavior Therapy*, 22, 1-12. Uses both popular and scholarly sources to describe some psychological consequences for persons whose body image differs markedly from what they perceive to be ideal. Enumerates several research and clinical implications regarding biological limitations, cultural ideals, and dieting.

262. Brumberg, J. (1988). *Fasting girls: The history of anorexia nervosa*. Cambridge: Harvard University Press.

Superb social history detailing popular culture influences on the recognition, incidence, and treatment of related eating disorders. The Victorian ideal of femininity was reflected by a slim body, and, in fact, some Victorians associated a thin female frame with a certain spirituality. Adolescent females continue to be encouraged in popular magazines to strive to be thin, so they will be perceived as more attractive. On the other hand, some elements of the press provide the public with the most personal details of the eating disorders of such celebrities like Karen Carpenter and Jane Fonda.

263. Diehl, L. (1986). The paradox of G. Stanley Hall: Foe of coeducation and educator of women. *American Psychologist*, 41, 868-878.

G. Stanley Hall, leader of functionalist psychology and one of the great organizers of American psychology, was a frequent contributor to popular magazines on topics ranging from masturbation to the nature of women. Using his position as a leader of psychology, Hall made numerous pronouncements against coeducation.

The author of this article argues that although Clark University (where Hall was president) was relatively open to female graduate students, Hall was most likely not confronted with strong feminist opposition from these same students. Such opposition might have caused him to question his sexist doctrine, which, apparently, he did not do.

264. Ehrenreich, B., and English, D. (1978). *For her own good: 150 years of experts' advice to women.* Garden City, NY: Anchor Press/Doubleday.
        Penetrating historical treatment of the role of "experts" in dispensing advice and analysis to American women. Much of this advice, a reflection of sexist ideology, comes across as patronizing and as an effort to deny the inhibiting aspects of the socio-political environment, which results in a trivialization of the concerns of women. Particularly relevant are the last three chapters, which center on the child and "masochistic motherhood." A section devoted to popular psychology is included.

265. Ehrenreich, B., Hess, E., and Jacobs, G. (1986). *Re-making love: The feminization of sex.* Garden City, NY: Anchor Press/Doubleday.
        Traces changes in female erotic practices and attitudes, resulting from the so-called sexual revolution of the latter half of the twentieth-century. Variations of traditional sexual behaviors have been communicated via popular media from such diverse sources as feminists, research physicians, sociologists, fundamentalist Christians, and popular psychologists. Articles, books, radio

and television programs, all suggest that contemporary women have sexual choices and that modern women often behave in ways not unlike their male partners. While the authors celebrate many of the changes that have contributed to a fuller expression of female sexuality, they express concern over the vulnerabilities of women in a culture still largely patriarchal, which leaves women often lacking opportunities for social and economic independence.

266. Faludi, S. (1991). *Backlash: The undeclared war against American women.* NY: Crown Publishers.

Impeccably researched study of attacks on feminism and women occurring in the 1980's. An entire chapter is devoted to popular psychological messages that blame women for all of their problems, especially those involving men. Includes discussion of numerous self-help books as well as radio psychology. There is additional analysis of the popularizations of the so-called Men's Movement, specifically the work of poet Robert Bly.

267. Furumoto, L. (1987). On the margins: Women and the professionalization of psychology in the United States, 1890-1940, in Mitchell Ash and William Woodward (Eds.), *Psychology in twentieth-century thought and society* (pp. 93-113). Cambridge: Cambridge University Press.

Includes a discussion of the life and works of Ethel Puffer Howes, whose academic career was destroyed by marriage and parenthood. Formerly a faculty member at Wellesley, Howes wrote two articles in 1922, which appeared in the *Atlantic Monthly.* She discussed the terrible choice facing women regarding career or marriage. Apparently, these articles were quite influential and led to the development of the Institute for the Coordination of Women's Interests at Smith College under the direction of Howes.

268. Koester, J. (1982). The Machiavellian princess: Rhetorical dramas for women managers, *Communication Quarterly*, 30, 165-172.

Views popular books for women managers as presenting a "vision" of success which offers conflicting messages. For example, aspiring women are told to be "feminine but not seductive" (p. 169) but given few if any concrete examples. Women are instructed to manage their image, so that they can attain the delicate balance mandated by the ambiguities of the organizational setting.

269. Rittenhouse, C. (1991). The emergence of premenstrual syndrome as a social problem, *Social Problems*, 38, 412-425.

Utilizing a content analysis of popular, medical, and feminist literature, the author demonstrates how PMS became a social problem. Apparently popular articles on the subject began to appear in 1954 with only twenty-four such articles showing up between that time and 1980. Criticism from feminist sources may have helped to reduce some of the more extreme portrayals of women with PMS as described in popular sources.

270.   Ross, E. (1980). "The love crisis": Couples advice
        books of the late 1970's, *Signs: Journal of
        Women in Culture and Society*, 6, 109-122.
        Thoughtful feminist analysis of the social
significance of the marital advice books of the
period. The author views these popular tomes as
offering two types of solutions to the couples
crisis: a possible competitive marketplace of love
and relationship or a possible return to traditional
gender relationships. Ross writes that these books
are directed toward middle-class females who
perceive a need to develop skills for reaching
fulfillment in marriage. Symptomatic of female
frustration is the heroine of Judy Blume's *Wifey*,
who voraciously reads and then implements a
variety of techniques aimed at communication and
sexual improvement.

271.   Simonds, W. (1992). *Women and self-help culture:
        Reading between the lines.* New
        Brunswick, NJ: Rutgers University Press.
        This book represents a major contribution to
the scholarly treatment of popular self-help
psychology books. Simonds interviewed thirty
female consumers of self-help texts as the basis for
a qualitative sociological analysis. She offers
preliminary answers in response to questions of
why women read such books, the relationships
between religious/spiritual concerns and self-help
reading, the role of editors and authors as well as
sexual and gender issues. A delightful chapter
chronicles reader reactions to Betty Friedan's *The
Feminine Mystique* and Robin Norwood's *Women
Who Love Too Much*. In a concluding chapter,
Simonds suggests that: "Reading self-help. . . is

about alienation and hope; about personal dissatisfaction and societal inadequacy; about wanting to conform to achieve magical happiness and about wanting to create new arrangements" (p. 226).

272. Simonds, W., and Rothman, B. (1992). *Centuries of solace: Expressions of maternal grief in popular literature.* Philadelphia: Temple University Press.

Offers a well-crafted view of the popular maternal consolation literature of the last two centuries. Analyzes around two hundred articles from nineteenth-century women's periodicals, surveys seventy-one items from the confessional magazine, *True Story,* and provides commentary on advice garnered from mass market tomes of the 1970's and 1980's. Included are numerous excerpts from the popular literature.

273. Smith-Rosenberg, C. (1972). The hysterical woman: Sex roles and role conflict in 19th-century America, *Social Research,* 39, 652-678.

Nineteenth-century advice manuals describe contradictory images of the ideal woman and the ideal mother. The former is to be both gentle and dependent, while the latter is to be self-reliant. Differing societal messages as well as changes permeating Victorian America certainly contributed to the psychopathologies of the day.

274. Wood, A. (1973). "The fashionable diseases": Women's complaints and their treatment in

nineteenth-century America, *The Journal of Interdisciplinary History*, 4, 25-52. Much of the popular medical advice, as well as much of the fiction of the nineteenth century, depicts women as delicate, nervous creatures, and captives of the uterus. Earlier in the century, around 1830-1860, for the treatment of nervous disorders, some women received "local treatment," which potentially could go through four stages: a manual adjustment, "leeching," "injections," and "cauterization." Later physicians, like S. Weir Mitchell prescribed "rest cures" and overfeeding, apparently obtaining "better results."

Popular Psychology Techniques

This section centers on writings which concern specific approaches to self-help. Most of the items discuss books and pamphlets, but some refer to audiotapes, videotapes, machines, and tests. Included is a sampling of citations covering a wide range of behavior-change topics such as career development, depression, sexuality, smoking cessation, and stress management.

275. Allen, D., and Workman, G. (1989). An interdepartmental self-management lab: A self-help approach to student development, *Journal of Counseling & Development*, 68, 106-108.
Describes a self-management lab located in the undergraduate library at the University of Illinois at Urbana-Champaign, which includes self-help books, audiotapes, videotapes, pamphlets, articles, and handouts on topics ranging from time management to women's health issues.

276. Andrasik, F., and Murphy, W. (1977). Assessing the readability of thirty-nine behavior modification training manuals and primers, *Journal of Applied Behavior Analysis*, 10, 341-344.
Analyzed readability of both popular and technical books. Using Flesch's Reading Ease Formula, the authors found that a number of the books written for general consumption were written at the seventh- to ninth-grade reading level.

277. Christensen, A., Miller, W., and Munoz, R. (1978). Paraprofessionals, partners, peers, paraphernalia, and print: Expanding mental health service delivery, *Professional Psychology*, 2, 249-270.
In their model for the expansion of service delivery, the authors delineate five types of therapeutic agents, two of which involve popular psychology: paraphernalia and print. Paraphernalia might include audiotapes covering typical life problems, while print could involve self-change

guides. Calls for empirical evaluation of all types of agents including self-help manuals.

278. Druckman, D., and Bjork, R. (1991). *In the mind's eye: Enhancing human performance.* Washington D.C.: National Academy Press. Presents findings from a National Research Council study of subliminal self-help audio tapes, self-assessment techniques for career planning, meditation practices, pain-management strategies, and sports-psychology techniques. Among the findings from this U.S. Army-sponsored research project is a lack of theoretical and empirical support demonstrating the efficacy of subliminal self-help, insufficient evidence supporting the Myers-Briggs Type Indicator (a popular self-assessment instrument) in career counseling and the effectiveness of non-pharmacological pain-management techniques

279. Ellis, A. (1978). Rational-emotive therapy and self-help therapy, *Rational Living,* 13, 3-8. Originally presented as part of an American Psychological Association symposium on non-prescriptive psychotherapies, chaired by Gerald Rosen. Ellis takes issue with the term "nonprescription therapy." Argues in favor of self-help therapy, especially his own brand, Rational Emotive Therapy. Includes five research hypotheses based on the author's clinical experience.

280. Glasgow, R., Schafer, L., and O'Neill, H. (1981). Self-help books and amount of therapist

contact in smoking cessation programs. *Journal of Consulting and Clinical Psychology*, 49, 659-667.
Describes an evaluation study of two self-help books aimed at smoking cessation under conditions of self-administration and therapist administration.

281. Gould, S. (1991). The import of Asian psycho-technologies into the United States: The "new woman" and the "new man" go "tantric," *Journal of American Culture*, 14, 19-23.
Eastern sexual psychotechnologies, like "Seminal and Ovarian Kung Fu," are entering American culture through New Age magazines, books, and videos. Asian philosophies when applied to lovemaking may serve to enhance love and physical attractiveness and through self-control (i.e. refraining from orgasm over long periods of time) may move participants in the direction of altered states. The author points out several cultural beliefs which may serve to block the diffusion of Asian transcendental sexual practices in America. Gould suggests that these psychotechnologies can contribute to increased sexual fulfillment with a monogamous partner.

282. Greenwald, A, Spangenber, E., Pratkanis, A., and Eskenazi, J. (1991). Double-blind tests of subliminal self-help audiotapes, *Psychological Science*, 2, 119-122.
Well-designed empirical examination of audiotapes claiming to enhance memory or increase

self-esteem. In three replications, the authors failed to substantiate the claims made by the tapes' manufacturers. However, a placebo effect did occur in that over a third of the subjects "had the illusion of improvement" (p. 119).

283. Hochschild, A. (1983). *The managed heart: The commercialization of human feeling.* Berkeley: University of California Press.
Delightful examination of how certain occupational groups, specifically airline stewards and stewardesses, are called upon to routinely manage personal feelings as an ongoing job requirement. Included are vivid descriptions of the use of popular psychological tactics in recurring staff development workshops.

284. Kanfer, F., and Gaelick, L. (1986). Self-management methods, in Frederick Kanfer and Arnold Goldstein (Eds.), *Helping People Change* (3rd edition) (pp. 283-345). New York: Pergamon Press.
Self-help resources are defined as "instructional materials and support groups that are designed to facilitate or maintain behavior change without the direct involvement of a mental health professional" (p. 33). Although problems with such materials are cited (e.g., lack of validity, a wide variance in quality, etc.), the authors describe three significant uses of self-help materials in the context of self-management. Literature which inspires and illustrates successful application of a program may reinforce the client's commitment; some self-help material may expose the client to a

wide variety of situations in which to consider the application of new behavioral skills; and such popular works may be used to learn specific skills related to assertiveness, relaxation, sexual responsiveness, and so forth.

285. Mahalik, J., and Kivlighan, Jr., D. (1988). Self-help treatment for depression: Who succeeds? *Journal of Counseling Psychology*, 35, 237-242.

Describes research with fifty-two mildly depressed undergraduates using a self-help manual with a cognitive-behavioral orientation. Results indicate that subjects scoring high on a scale measuring realism were most successful with self-help, while those labeled as enterprising had the least success.

286. Orleans, T., Schoenbach, V., Wagner, E., Quade, D., Salmon, M., Pearson, D., Fiedler, J., Porter, C., and Kaplan, B. (1990). Self-help quit smoking interventions: Effects of self-help materials, social support instructions, and telephone counseling, *Journal of Consulting and Clinical Psychology*, 59, 439-448.

Well-designed evaluation research showing some positive effects of self-help materials for smoking cessation.

287. Register, A., May, J., Beckham, J., and Gustafson, D. (1991). Stress inoculation in the treatment of test anxiety. *Journal of Counseling Psychology*, 38, 115-119.

Supports the effectiveness of bibliotherapy for reducing symptoms related to test anxiety in college students. A very high percentage (ninety-four percent) of subjects completed the manual, which is much higher than the usual rate of adherence.

288. Risse, G. (1976). Vocational guidance during the Depression: Phrenology versus applied psychology, *Journal of the History of the Behavioral Sciences*, 12, 130-140.

Entertaining description of the psychograph, a machine concocted in 1930 as a means of assessing mental traits according to phrenological principles. Donald Paterson and Richard Elliot of the University of Minnesota publicly assailed the psychograph, and Paterson did so during a radio talk in 1931. Although the psychograph was utilized by a few firms for vocational counseling, it never became popular. Interestingly, the psychograph was displayed at the 1933 World's Fair adjacent to a flea show "and a real two-headed baby in a formalin-filled bottle" (p. 138). Risse argues that reliable mental testing had received the support of the American public, making phrenological techniques anachronistic.

289. Scogin, F., Hamblin, D., and Beutler, L. (1987). Bibliotherapy for depressed older adults: A self-help alternative, *The Gerontologist*, 27, 383-387.

Preliminary analysis of cognitive self-help bibliotherapy with mildly to moderately depressed older adults, which demonstrates significant reduction in depression according to self- and observer ratings.

290. Scogin, F., Jamison, C., and Davis, N. (1990). Two-year follow-up of bibliotherapy for depression in older adults, *Journal of Consulting and Clinical Psychology*, 58, 665-667.
Results of this study reinforce the findings of Scogin et al. (1989). The authors caution the reader since only thirty of the forty original subjects participated, assessments in the present study were made by telephone, and a control condition was not used.

291. Scogin, F., Jamison, C., and Gochneaur, K. (1989). Comparative efficacy of cognitive and behavioral bibliotherapy for mildly and moderately depressed older adults, *Journal of Consulting and Clinical Psychology*, 57, 403-407.
Found both behavioral and cognitive bibliotherapy to be equally effective. Those participating in the behavioral condition were to read *Control Your Depression*, while those in the cognitive condition were given a copy of *Feeling Good*.

292. Swets, J., and Bjork, R. (1990). Enhancing human performance: An evaluation of "new age" techniques considered by the U.S. Army, *Psychological Science*, 1, 85-96.
Highly readable description of the activities of the Committee on Techniques for the Enhancement of Human Performance selected by the

National Research Council. The Army desired a scientific analysis of the validity and possible utility of a number of performance-enhancing strategies. The committee's findings reflect a great deal of skepticism regarding many of the claims of commercial promoters of many techniques, including those involving learning during sleep, neurolinguistic programming, and parapsychological phenomena. Interestingly, Swets and Bjork write that: "The committee observed a pervasive army tendency to accept and implement enhancement techniques on the basis of personal or clinical experience and marketplace popularity instead of on the basis of research evidence" (p. 92). The article includes a description of the public reaction to the publication of the committee's first book, and the resulting political machinations.

293. Watson, D., and Tharp, R., (1989). *Self-directed behavior: Self-modification for personal adjustment* (5th edition). Pacific Grove, CA: Brooks/Cole.

Constructed for use in psychology of adjustment courses or for self-directed behavior change. Do-it-yourself behavior modification is coupled with a thorough listing of primary references of self-management research.

Critiques of Popular Psychology

This final section of bibliographic entries reflects criticism of American popular psychology in the context of the larger culture. Much of the social commentary lambastes Americans for being self-indulgent, lacking critical judgment, and searching for easy and painless solutions to complex problems. Assessments come from a variety of political viewpoints ranging from Edwin Schur's left-of-center position which views the self-absorption of self-help psychology as a diversion from sorely needed social change to Paul Vitz's rightist views of popular self-psychology as "self-worship."

294. Albee, G. (1977). The Protestant ethic, sex, and psychotherapy, *American Psychologist*, 32, 150-161.

Sees the development in America of an indulgent society. Argues that a society based on consumption has gnawed away at the fundamental values inherent in the Protestant ethic. As an example of value change, Albee recounts having picked up a *Redbook* magazine and being surprised to find an article touting the utility of the vibrator for masturbation. Thrashes students of the 1970's as "members of the Pepsi Generation," who "cannot discipline themselves" (p. 160). Albee refers to the popularity of such books as the *Joy of Sex* and *Sex Without Guilt* as reflective of self-indulgence.

295. Cannel, W., and Macklin, J. (1974). *The human nature industry: How human nature is manufactured, distributed, advertised, and consumed in the United States and parts of Canada.* Garden City, NY: Anchor Press/Doubleday.

This tongue-in-cheek offering from a journalist and anthropologist includes a wide assortment of barbs meant for many segments of North American culture including the human nature experts. The authors appear to be saying that people construct models of human nature to know what to do in order to manage their lives. Through the human nature industry, a myriad of messages are received, and the authors warn that: "Human nature will be what the loudest, most coercive voice says it is" (p. 285).

296. Cushman, P. (1992). Psychotherapy to 1992: A historically situated interpretation, in Donald Freedheim (Ed.), *History of psychotherapy: A century of change* (pp. 21-64). Washington, D.C.: American Psychological Association.

In an extension of his 1990 *American Psychologist* article, Cushman traces the sociohistorical context of therapy from mesmerism through the late twentieth century and concludes that there are three highly significant themes in the history of psychotherapy: advertising and consumerism, the role of therapy in the healing of personal interiority, and psychology's rationalization and methodologies for interacting with the empty self. This well-written chapter includes numerous examples of the interaction of currents in popular culture with psychology and psychotherapy. A strong reference list adds to the chapter's value.

297. Cushman, P. (1990). Why the self is empty: Toward a historically situated psychology, *American Psychologist*, 45, 599-611.

The author asserts that a number of American industries arose to treat the emerging "empty self." Among these industries has been that of the self-improvement enterprise, which, according to Cushman, is comprised of "mainstream psychology, pop psychology, and pop religion" (p. 604). The development of this self-improvement industry may be due to a sense of meaninglessness and emptiness in the general populace.

298. Jacoby, R. (1975). *Social amnesia: A critique of
      conformist psychology from Adler to Laing.*
      Boston: Beacon Press.
      Social criticism of those who deem
      themselves to be radical psychological reformers.
      Clever passages tear at T-groups and humanistic
      psychologists. Jacoby's pointed style rings clear
      when he writes: "One helps oneself because
      collective help is inadmissible; in rejecting the
      realm of social and political praxis, individual
      helplessness is redoubled and soothes itself through
      self-help, hobbies, and how-to manuals" (p. 51).

299. Kaminer, W. (1992). *I'm dysfunctional, you're
      dysfunctional: The recovery movement and
      other self-help fashions.* Reading, MA:
      Addison-Wesley.
      A witty, sarcastic slap at various attempts at
      self-help. Kaminer cleverly jabs at the simplicities
      and hyperboles of the recovery movement, positive
      thinking, support groups, New Age strategies, est,
      and the covenant between pop theology and pop
      psychology. Passionately pleading with the reader
      to utilize critical thinking and analysis, Kaminer in
      concluding remarks states that: "Self-help books
      market authority in a culture that idealizes
      individualism but not thinking and fears the
      isolation of being free" (p. 165).

300. Lasch, C. (1977). *The culture of narcissism.*
      New York: W. W. Norton.
      Lasch points both barrels of his critical
      weapon at aspects of popular psychology such as
      Parent Effectiveness Training and open marriage,

which encourage people to feel and not think. Psychological men and women attempt to insulate themselves from others; others are significant only to the degree that they impact the self. The narcissistic personality strives to manipulate others, while attempting to maintain control. In an effort to distinguish value judgments from "objective truths," social scientists have often encouraged the "devaluation of values," which encourages consumers of social science pronouncements in their efforts toward self-aggrandizement and detachment.

301. Lasch, C. (1984). *The minimal self: Psychic survival in troubled times.* New York: Norton.

Essentially, this book is an extension of the author's earlier masterwork, *The Culture of Narcissism.* Lasch continues to view self-oriented strategies like "nonbinding commitments" as developing out of "the culture of consumption" (p. 18), and he wonders whether a more apt description of our situation might be a "culture of survivalism" (p. 57).

302. Rieff, P. (1966). *The triumph of the therapeutic: Uses of faith after Freud.* New York: Harper & Row.

Scholars are especially encouraged to examine the introduction and the final chapter. The book is replete with insights regarding popular culture and psychological themes.

303. Rosen, R. (1977). *Psychobabble.* New York: Atheneum.

Journalist Rosen takes trendy psychological talk and technique apart. Devotes chapters to the work of David Viscott ("Sensitivity, Inc."), Werner Erhard (est), Harvey Jackins (co-counseling), Kenneth Mark Colby (computer therapy), Leonard Orr (rebirthing), and Arthur Janov (primal therapy). Criticizes American culture as "swimming in quick methods of understanding and changing human behavior...psychobabble represents the rejection of narration in favor of psychological ad copy" (p. 212). In a concluding chapter, Rosen describes transactional analysis in somewhat less critical fashion. The message of the book is reflected in the final sentence: "The problem is not that so many are constantly looking for enlightenment these days, but that so many are constantly finding it" (p. 230).

304. Rosenman, S. (1976). Popular psychology and personality theory, *American Journal of Psychoanalysis*, 36, 43-56.

This article contains a stinging critique of an immensely popular book entitled, *How To Be Your Own Best Friend*, by psychoanalysts M. Newman and B. Berkowitz. Rosenman believes that the authors of this self-help guide unknowingly encouraged their readers to sever their healthy attachments to others by centering exclusively on self, and he perceives another limiting factor of the Newman and Berkowitz text to be its avoidance of the concept of evil both within the individual and in the world.

305. Schur, E. (1976). *The awareness trap: Self-absorption instead of social change.* New

York: Quadrangle.

The author provides a thoughtful critique of the self-awareness movement. Chapters cover "Feeling Your Feelings," "Achieving Sensory Success," "Learning to be Real," "The Mystique of Relating," "Women and Awareness," and "Therapy More or Less." Schur argues that the themes of the movement are consistent with traditional American values of personal responsibility and individualism but that this same movement encourages persons to seek simple, quick answers to rather profound problems. As the title of the text implies, such self-concern may discourage many from seeking constructive social change.

306. Sennett, R. (1977). *The fall of public man.* New York: Alfred A. Knopf.

Broad critique of American culture which includes material on psychology's impact.

307. Vitz, P. (1977). *Psychology as religion: The cult of self-worship.* Grand Rapids, MI: William B. Eerdmans Publishing Company.

Written by a psychology professor from N.Y.U., this book is essentially a Christian critique of the popular self-psychology of the 1970's. Vitz slings arrows at Fromm, Rogers, Maslow, and May and not only castigates each of them for promoting self-oriented ideas about human nature but states that none of them "is likely to merit consideration as a major thinker" (p. 28). The author particularly outraged at the excesses of such self-theories and therapies as est, assertiveness training, open marriage, and transactional analysis. The author rails against the evils of secular humanism and prescribes fundamental Christianity for all.

308. Wachtel, P. (1983). *The poverty of affluence: A psychological portrait of the American way of life.* New York: The Free Press.

Writing as both psychologist and social analyst, Wachtel not only takes American society to task but slings arrows at such social critics as Lasch and Schur. The author argues that the crass materialism of the larger culture leads to a vacuous existence and is a natural outcome of individualism and isolationism. Included is a clever commentary on some of the excesses of the human potential movement.

309. Wallach, M. and Wallach, L. (1983). *Psychology's sanction for selfishness: The error of egoism in theory and therapy.* San Francisco: W. H. Freeman and Company.

Presents a cogent argument that psychology as a discipline has fostered a self-centered view of humanity. Popular psychologies like encounter and assertion training and approaches to social behavior like exchange theory emphasize the selfish nature of humanity. An egoistic perspective is found in most general textbooks, personality theories, and professional therapies. The Wallachs argue that scientific research reflecting a more socially concerned human is underrepresented in both popular and "scientific" summaries of the literature, and they describe personal and societal benefits that accrue when people are encouraged to behave in a caring fashion.

310. West, L. and Singer, M. (1980). Cults, quacks, and nonprofessional psycho-therapies. In H. Kaplan, A. Freedman, and B. Sadock (Eds.), *Comprehensive textbook of psychiatry* (Vol. 3) (pp. 3245-3258). Baltimore, MD: Williams and Wilkins.

Interesting to note is the title of this chapter which places nonprofessional (roughly equated with popular) psychotherapies on a par with cults and quacks. The authors note the basically benign nature of many forms of self-improvement but warn against the risks implicit in such interventions. The so-called benefits of these treatments may be a reflection of the placebo effect.

Afterword: Research Ideas in American Popular Psychology

Reviewing the scholarly and professional literature on popular psychology gives rise to numerous researchable notions. The interdisciplinary nature of the subject contributes both to a variety of ways of assessing the current state of knowledge as well as to a host of topics and issues in need of further examination. Researchers from the fields of psychology, sociology, American and popular culture studies, history, journalism, or education may wish to investigate some of the following questions:

(1)   Why does some popular psychology continue to be widely received for a relatively long period of time (e.g., the works of Dale Carnegie, Norman Vincent Peale, Benjamin Spock, and M. Scott Peck), while other efforts are soon forgotten?

(2)   What are the relationships between formal psychological theory and research, the professional practice of psychology, and popular psychology? What effects do each of these have on the others? For example, do some ideas which appear to originate in popular psychology eventually give rise to theory and research or to changes in professional practice?

(3)   How have non-Christians (e.g., Jews, Muslims, secular humanists, and so forth) interpreted the explicitly Christian messages of the success and the recovery movements?

(4)   In what ways has popular psychology (e.g., articles from *Psychology Today* have been required reading in some courses) been utilized in undergraduate psychology education?

(5) How are popular psychological concepts (e.g., dysfunctional families) communicated in undergraduate textbooks in fields other than psychology (e.g., communications, management, and so forth)?

(6) What role does popular psychology play in the curriculum of seminaries and in the continuing education activities of American clergy?

(7) What ever became of Transactional Analysis (TA)? Is it still popular? Through what channels are the precepts of TA being disseminated? What happened to the leaders of the movement?

(8) How has the magazine *Psychology Today* weathered the 1960's, 1970's, 1980's, and the early 1990's?

(9) Why did the Myers-Briggs instrument become popularized?

(10) How do journalists determine if an individual is an expert on psychological matters?

(11) How do consumers make decisions on which popular psychology books to purchase?

(12) How do television talk shows covering psychological topics affect public attitudes and mental health practices?

(13) How have diverse cultural groups been addressed in the popular psychology literature?

APPENDIXES

Appendix 1

Chronology of Events in the History of American Psychology

1710	Publication of Cotton Mathers' *Bonifacius: Essays to Do Good*
1732-1757	Publication of Benjamin Franklin's *Poor Richard's Almanac*
1820's	Charles Poyen begins American lectures on hypnotism
1838	George Combe begins lecturing on phrenology across the northeastern United States
1849	Orson Fowler and his associates publish *Phrenology Proved, Illustrated, and Applied....*
1881	Publication of George Beard's *American Nervousness: Its Causes and Consequences*
1882	Herbert Spencer begins his American lecture tour in which he promotes Social Darwinism

1890	Publication of William James' *The Principles of Psychology*
1893	Psychology exhibits at the Chicago World's Fair, including a testing laboratory and research apparatus
1900	Publication of Sigmund Freud's *The Interpretation of Dreams*
1900-1902	Publication of *Practical Psychology*, a periodical for laypersons
1904	Psychology exhibits and lecture by such notables as E. B. Titchener, G. S. Hall, and J. B. Watson at the Louisiana Purchase Exposition in St. Louis
1908	Publication of *A Mind That Found Itself* by Clifford Beers, a former psychiatric patient
1909	Sigmund Freud and Carl Jung lecture at Clark University in Worcester, Massachusetts
1914	The U.S. Department of Labor initiates publication of the pamphlet, *Infant Care*
1920-1930	J. B. Watson writes numerous popular articles in magazines like *Harper's*
1920-1930	Psychologist Grace Adams writes popular articles criticizing both the popularization of psychology and the gullibility of the general public
1922-1923	Journalist Walter Lippmann writes a series of articles for the *New Republic*, in which he criticizes the Army intelligence tests as well as some psychologists
1923	Psychologist Robert Yerkes tells readers of the *Atlantic Monthly* of the "reality" of racial differences in intelligence
1928	Publication of J. B. Watson's *Psychological Care of the Infant and Child*

1935	Founding of Alcoholics Anonymous
1936	Publication of Dale Carnegie's *How to Win Friends and Influence People*
1945	B. F. Skinner writes an article for the *Ladies' Home Journal* on his air-crib
1946	Publication of Benjamin Spock's *The Pocket Book of Baby and Child Care*
1947	Psychologist Lewis Terman appears on the "Quiz Kids" radio program
1948	Publication of *Walden II*, B. F. Skinner's novel of a behavioral utopia
1952	Publication of Norman Vincent Peale's *The Power of Positive Thinking*
1967	*Psychology Today* begins publication
1967	Publication of Thomas Harris's *I'm OK, You're OK*
1968	George Miller's presidential address to the American Psychological Association challenging his constituents "to give psychology away"
1970's	The first call-in radio psychology programs begin in California
1974	The American Psychological Association establishes an office of public information
1978	Publication of M. Scott Peck's *The Road Less Traveled*
1983	The American Psychological Association purchases *Psychology Today*
1987	Publication of Melody Beattie's *Codependent No More: How to Stop Controlling Others and Start Caring for Yourself*
1990	Publication of Robert Bly's *Iron John: A Book About Men*

Appendix 2

Self-help Psychology Bestsellers of 1990, 1991, and 1992

1990

*Hardcover

Ranking	Title	#Weeks on 1990 List
1	You Just Don't Understand: Men and Women in Conversation	21
2	Homecoming: Reclaiming and Championing Your Inner Child	20
3	Secrets about Men Every Woman Should Know	19

* *Publisher's Weekly*, January 4, 1991, p. 44.

1990

*Trade Paperback

Ranking	Title	#Weeks on 1990 List
1	Codependent No More	51
2	Dianetics: Revised Edition	21
3	The Road Less Traveled	14

* *Publisher's Weekly*, January, 4, 1991, p. 45.

1991

*Hardcover

Ranking	Title	#Weeks on 1990 List
1	Iron John: A Book About Men	47
2	Homecoming	31
3	Fire in the Belly: On Being a Man	18

* *Publisher's Weekly*, January 1, 1992, p. 34.

1991

*Trade Paperback

Ranking	Title	#Weeks on 1990 List
1	7 Habits of Highly Effective People	48
2	Codependent No More	32
3	You Just Don't Understand: Men and Women in Conversation	30

* *Publisher's Weekly*, January 1, 1992, p. 35.

1991

*Hardcover

Ranking	Title	#Weeks on 1990 List
1	How to Satisfy a Woman Every Time	35
2	A Return to Love	32
3	The Silent Passage: Menopause	27

* *Publisher's Weekly*, January 4, 1993, p. 50.

Appendix 3

Recent Self-Help Psychology Bestsellers: A Preliminary Analysis

Sharon Barfield and Stephen Fried

An earlier version of this paper was presented at the Fifteenth Annual Meeting of the American Culture Association, April 9, 1993, New Orleans, Louisiana.

Popular self-help psychology has a long and rich tradition in the United States. According to Robert Fuller, "popular psychology refers to those writings specifically addressed to general reading audiences" (22, p. 173). Early American self-help guides were penned by both religious leaders like Cotton Mather and secular ones such as Benjamin Franklin. By the late nineteenth-century, readers were able to choose from a wide assortment of publications reflecting the "gospel of success" or the "power to heal" (Starker, 191).

Self-help psychology books continue to have wide appeal. In response to a questionnaire given to a random sample of Chicago parents, K. Alison Clarke-Stewart (232) found that 94 percent had read at least one popular article or book on the care of children and that more than 44 percent of the mothers had read five or more such parenting books. Steven Starker (191) attributes the pervasive influence of these works to four key factors: cost, accessibility, privacy, and excitement. Popular psychology books are available for a fraction of the cost of one therapeutic hour, and they can be found in the local bookstore, library, or grocery store. Reading a book is a private affair, and one may identify with other persons who have read the secrets surrounding perfect parenting or sensuous marriage (Starker, 191).

Self-help psychology bestsellers have been written by mental health professionals as well as lay persons, and numerous psychologists and social commentators have been critical of this commercialization (Barrera, Rosen, and Glasgow, 171; Burnham, 12; Kaminer, 200; Rosen, 186, 187. Glasgow and Rosen (178) found that the overall ratio of supporting studies to behavioral self-help books decreased within a two-year period from .86 (74 studies for 86 programs) to .59 (43 studies for 73 programs). Gerald Rosen argued that psychologists have "published untested material, advanced exaggerated claims and accepted the use of misleading titles that encourage unrealistic expectations" (Rosen, 185). Rosen developed guidelines for the academic review of self-help treatment books; he also chaired a task force on self-help psychology for the American Psychological Association, and subsequently claimed that commercial considerations, not professional standards, have influenced the development of some treatment books and that consumers risk purchasing self-help books which may be ineffective or even harmful (Rosen, 186).

Several studies have demonstrated positive benefits associated with reading self-help materials. For example, using a pretest-posttest design, Forest (177) found that persons reading a self-help book on self-actualization demonstrated higher self-report scores in regards to two measures of actualization than did members of a control group. Depressed college students have been treated successfully with self-help manuals (Mahalik & Kivlighan, 286), and persons experiencing a recent divorce or other relationship dissolution have reported fewer symptoms associated with loss after utilizing self-help materials (Ogles, Lambert, & Craig, 183).

A number of psychologists and other mental health professionals appear to view self-help psychology books in a positive vein. Steven Starker (192) found that many health-care professionals recommend such books to their clients. Of those professionals queried, almost 90 percent of the psychologists, 60 percent of the psychiatrists, and around 85 percent of the internists indicated they read and prescribed such works to patients as a supplement to treatment. Subsequently Starker (190) examined the practice of bibliotherapy as an adjunct to therapy and found most of the participating psychologists satisfied with the quality and helpfulness of specific publications.

The present study considers the appearance and content of ten best-selling, popular psychology books.

Method

In order to develop a list of the top ten best-selling self-help psychology books of 1989, 1990, and 1991, we counted the the number of times each title appeared on the paperback bestseller list of *Publisher's Weekly* for the years in question. From this tabulation, a list of the top eight best-selling titles was made. In order to verify and expand the list, we also went through the same three years of *The New York Times Book Review*, counting the number of times each title appeared on that paperback bestseller list. The two lists were then compared yielding a total of ten book titles. In descending order of the number of appearances in the two sources, the titles are: *Codependent No More; The Road Less Traveled; The 7 Habits of Highly Effective People; You Just Don't Understand; Love, Medicine, and Miracles; Beyond Codependency; The Dance of Anger; Healing the Shame That Binds You; The Language of Letting Go;* and *Life 101.*

Utilizing criteria generated in part from Gerald Rosen's (185) guidelines as well as from other classification literature (Bonk & Carter, 1969; Katz, 1974), we analyzed the books using the following questions:

1.   Is the cover of the book eye-catching?
2.   Is the cover free of claims regarding the effectiveness of the contents?
3.   Is the purpose of the book clearly stated in the preface, introduction, or first chapter?
4.   Is the author a mental health professional?

5. Are contents of the book free of claims about the effectiveness of specific strategies?
6. Does the author attempt to convey information regarding empirical support for the strategies contained in the book?
7. Does the book outline a specific method of treatment?
8. Does the author include accounts of personal experience as the basis for the position taken?
9. Is the writing clear and coherent?
10. Does the book contain a bibliography?

Each of us analyzed the ten books independently, and we found ourselves in agreement 91 percent of the time. In those cases where we disagreed initially, we discussed our differences and reached a consensus.

Results and Discussion

The results of our analysis can be found in Table 1 on page 196.

Table 1

Criteria

Books	1	2	3	4	5	6	7	8	9	10
Codependent	Yes	No	Yes	No	No	No	Yes	Yes	No	Yes
The Road	Yes	No	No	Yes	No	No	Yes	Yes	Yes	Yes
Seven Habits	Yes	No	Yes	No	No	No	Yes	Yes	Yes	No
Don't Understand	Yes	No	Yes	No	Yes	Yes	No	Yes	Yes	Yes
Love Medicine	Yes	No	Yes	No	No	Yes	Yes	Yes	Yes	Yes
Beyond	Yes	No	Yes	Yes	Yes	No	Yes	Yes	No	Yes
Dance of Anger	Yes	No	Yes	Yes	No	No	Yes	Yes	Yes	Yes
Healing	Yes	No	Yes	Yes	No	No	Yes	Yes	No	Yes
Language	Yes	No	Yes	Yes	Yes	No	No	Yes	No	No
Life 101	Yes	No	No	No	Yes	No	No	Yes	No	No

Key:
  1 = Appearance   6 = Empirical
  2 = Claims   7 = Treatment
  3 = Purpose   8 = Experience
  4 = Author   9 = Coherent
  5 = Strategy   10 = Bibliography

The most popular book, Melody Beattie's *Codependent No More*, centers on codependents as "people tormented by other people's behavior" (p. 1). Such codependents are viewed as enablers who rescue others from responsibilities and then feel abused and sorry for themselves, making the situation even worse. Codependents are so involved with other people's problems that they neglect their own. The book includes several case histories detailing relationship problems, a five-page quiz so readers can determine if they, too, are codependent, as well as strategies for overcoming problems associated with dependency, anger, goal setting, and acceptance.

First published in 1978, M. Scott Peck's *The Road Less Traveled* continues its bestselling status. Philip Cushman (298) considers the self-improvement industry to be comprised of popular psychology, popular religion, and mainstream psychology, and Peck's book, which intertwines spiritual with psychological questions and answers, reflects all three of these elements. Spiritual and emotional issues are treated as one in this truly Christian guide to mental health. Self-discipline can be utilized to overcome the myriad of problems confronting life's travelers. In a populist afterword, Peck proclaims that: "A therapist's abilities bear very little relationship to any credentials he or she might have. Love and courage cannot be certified by academic degrees" (p. 314).

Another self-help book with a decidedly spiritual message is Stephen Covey's *The 7 Habits of Highly Effective People*. Covey offers what he suggests is a new paradigm for personal success and directs the reader to be proactive, plan ahead, prioritize, listen actively, synthesize, and self-develop continuously. Each chapter is replete with diagrams, and suggestions for real-world application are provided in the form of specific questions and activities which are aimed at engaging the reader. Just inside the front cover of the book the reader is accosted with seven pages of testimonials from CEO's, professional quarterbacks, a U.S. Senator, academics, and even Marie Osmond. Inside the back cover, readers are introduced to "Seven Habits" products (e.g., "The Seven Habits Executive Organizer"), which can be obtained through writing or calling the Covery Leadership Center.

You Just Don't Understand, written by Georgetown University Linguist Deborah Tannen, centers on communication problems between men and women. Because people with different backgrounds may have different conversational styles, the messages received are not always consistent with the meanings which are intended. Tannen's position reflects the notion that male-female relationship problems may, in part, be the result of the differing socialization experience afforded each gender. Different conversational styles can emerge from gender-oriented enculturation which can lead to mis-communication even in those instances when both parties are genuinely attempting to relate to one another in an egalitarian fashion. Tannen attempts to provide a general audience with a readable distillation of research covering an aspect of the cost of sexist socialization, full of academic and popular sources, a complete list of references, as well as a detailed index.

Surgeon Bernie Siegel offers a guide to the healing powers of the mind in *Love, Medicine and Miracles*. Siegel discusses his experience in treating cancer patients holistically in a manner which promotes personal change and healing. By instructing patients to develop a loving, peaceful attitude and to live fully in the present moment instead of centering on the horrors of the future, patients develop peace of mind. Through meditation, progressive relaxation, and guided imagery in which they write a personal script which may include healthy cells devouring cancerous ones, patients may utilize the powers of the mind in the healing process. Siegel believes that the mind receives sensory input when under anesthesia and suggests that when a patient's favorite music is played during surgery, the individual may experience a faster recovery and require less pain medication.

Beyond Codependency is another recovery book authored by Melody Beattie. The tone, message, and even the cover quite similar to her earlier blockbuster, *Codependent No More.* Those in recovery which might include, depending on one's definition, all of us, are instructed to affirm our positive aspects. The reader is provided with numerous activities through which self-affirmation will hopefully occur. In the manner of the "Saturday Night Live" character, Stuart Smalley, the reader is told to "Write a set of personalized affirmations. Write loving, empowering affirmations that feel good when you read them. Spend time each day reading these, saying them aloud... Take time, when you're looking in the mirror, to tell yourself you love you, you're beautiful, you're good at what you do" (p. 136). Repeatedly Beattie encourages the reader to seek God and support groups in the never ending struggle toward recovery.

Menninger Clinic psychologist Harriet Goldhor Lerner combines psychoanalytic, family systems, and feminist concepts in *The Dance of Anger*, which explores women's behavior. Lerner writes that because many women are socialized to play the part of the "Nice Lady;" they typically stay silent, become tearful, self-critical, or feel hurt in situations which could understandably evoke anger. The author offers four basic strategies for using anger as a constructive tool in relationships: (1) learn to determine the true source of one's anger, what the real issue is, and one's position is; (2) learn effective communication skills; (3) learn to observe and interrupt ineffective behaviors and interactions; and (4) learn to anticipate others. Included are several case histories in which anger is handled effectively.

John Bradshaw's *Healing The Shame That Binds You* is all about what he calls toxic shame, a term which is used throughout the book, over and over again. In fact, "toxic shame" appears five times in the acknowledgments section of the book alone. Writing as a fellow sufferer/ victim, Bradshaw sees such shame, as well as toxic guilt, as forming the foundation of human misery. Bits and pieces of psychological teachings are interwoven with religious themes, as Bradshaw proclaims that: "The problem of toxic shame is ultimately a spiritual problem" (p. 22). Bradshaw utilizes numerous graphs and charts aimed at assisting the reader in self-integration and in liberating a "lost inner child." The book is written as a testimony to the author's personal crises and healing as well as to his belief in 12-step programs. Bradshaw proclaims that nothing short of a spiritual awakening will heal one's toxic shame and the psychological dysfunction which he believes will result.

The Language of Letting Go is a book of meditations written expressly for codependents. Melody Beattie offers the reader brief passages meant to be read as self-affirmation. Pretty birds don the cover of this little book which is meant to be up-beat. In the introduction, Beattie proclaims that: "It is a book to help you feel good and assist you in the process of self-care and recovery" (Introduction). Most of the affirmations, which are about one page in length, exhort the reader to love self and God and to accept personal limitations, which is all consistent with the 12-step ideology.

The last bestseller, *Life 101*, written by John-Roger and Peter McWilliams, is a compilation of numerous suggestions and asides regarding what the authors call in the subtitle, "Everything We Wish We had Learned About Life in School - but Didn't." The book is somewhat difficult to follow. On the same otherwise blank page, quotes from Ward Cleaver and Lily Tomlin appear seeming to suggest that the reader can gain some real insight from them. Could the authors be playing a highly profitable joke on the unsuspecting and befuddled readers? In a four-page section preceding the index, readers are informed about seminars, degree programs, audiotapes, even *Life 101* wristwatches which may be purchased from the authors. A pocket-size *Life 101* is also available at bookstores for ready reference and inspiration.

This preliminary look at ten self-help bestsellers provides a series of impressions. Without exception, the books are packaged attractively with eye-catching cover designs. Claims are made on the cover of each book which are frequently left unfulfilled by the book's contents. Typically, the purpose is stated, and claims are made about the given book's effectiveness. Most of the authors do not utilize empirical support for their assertions, which is surprising given the fact that the authors of five of the books have training on the doctoral level. A number of books offer specific methods of treatment with the most frequent one following the 12-step model. Authors rely heavily on their own personal suffering as well as professional experience. Although four authors function as mental health professionals, specific academic degree information is not given for two of the four. Some of the writing is quite disjointed and almost unedited (e.g., *Life 101*). Interestingly, seven of the books do contain a bibliography.

We have some general impressions of the content and style of these popular works. Spiritual themes are rampant in all but two books, *The Dance of Anger* and *You Just Don't Understand*, which reflect a more secular bent. Four of the works focus on recovery and codependency, all of which were penned by recovering substance abusers/ codependents. Several books approach more general themes of increasing personal happiness by achieving success through more effective goal setting and inter-personal relationships. The advice given is quite general and often ambiguous with the reader exhorted to trust self and to trust God!

Regardless of the effectiveness of the recommendations or the quality of the prose, self-help psychology books continue to sell. Wendy Simonds (272) reports on the reason why so many American women consume self-help books in *Women and Self-Help Culture: Reading Between the Lines*. One of those persons interviewed confides to Simonds: "I thought they had the answers. And I still do, in some stupid way. Rationally, I know these books don't have the answers; emotionally, I really think if I find the right book, it will solve my problems" (p. 1).

The quest for answers to personal problems through self-help psychology books continues.

References

Barrera, M., Rosen, G., & Glasgow, R. (1981). Rights, risks, and responsibilities in the use of self-help psychotherapy. In G. Hannah, W. Christian, & H. Clark (Eds.), *Preservation of client rights: A handbook for practitioners providing therapeutic, educational, and rehabilitative services* (pp. 204-220). New York: The Free Press.

Beattie, M. (1987). *Codependent no more: How to stop controlling others and start caring for yourself.* New York: Harper & Row.

Beattie, M. (1989). *Beyond codependence: And getting better all the time.* New York: Harper & Row.

Beattie, M. (1990). *The language of letting go: Daily meditations for codependents.* New York: Harper/ Collins.

Bonk, W. J. & Carter, M. D. (1969). *Building library collections.* Metuchen, NJ: Scarecrow Press.

Bradshaw, J. (1988). *Healing the shame that binds you.* Deerfield Beach, FL: Health Communications.

Burnham, J. C. (1987). *How superstition won and science lost.* New Brunswick: Rutgers University Press.

Clarke-Stewart, K. A. (1978). Popular primers for parents. *American Psychologist,* 33, 359-369.

Covey, S. R. (1989). *The 7 habits of highly effective people: Powerful lessons in personal change.* New York: Simon and Schuster.

Forest, J. J. (1987). Effects of self-actualization of paperbacks. *Psychological Reports,* 60, 1243-1246.

Fuller, R. (1986). *Americans and the unconscious.* New York: Oxford University Press.

Glasgow, R. E. & Rosen, G. M. (1978). Behavioral bibliotherapy: A review of self-help behavior therapy manuals. *Psychological Bulletin,* 85, 1-23.

Glasgow, R. E. & Rosen, G. M. (1979). Self-help behavior therapy manuals: Recent developments and clinical usage. *Clinical Behavior Therapy Review,* 1, 1-20.

John-Roger & McWilliams, P. (1991). *Life 101.* Los Angeles: Prelude Press.

Kaminer, W. (1992). *I'm dysfunctional, you're dysfunctional.* Reading: Addison-Wesley Publishing.

Katz, W. A. (1974). *Introduction to reference work: Vol 1. Basic information sources* (2nd ed.). New York: McGraw-Hill.

Lerner, H. G. (1989). *The dance of anger: A woman's guide to changing the pattern of intimate relationships.* New York: Harper & Row.

Mahalik, J. R. & Kivlighan, D. M. (1988). Self-help treatment for depression: who succeeds? *Journal of Counseling Psychology, 35,* 237-242.

Ogles, B. M., Lambert, M. J., & Craig, D. E. (1991). Comparison of self-help books for coping with loss: expectations and attributions. *Journal of Counseling Psychology, 4,* 387-393.

Peck, M. S. (1978). *The road less traveled: A new psychology of love, traditional values and spiritual growth.* New York: Simon & Schuster.

Rosen, G. M. (1976). The development and use of nonprescription behavior therapies. *American Psychologist, 31,* 139-141.

Rosen, G. M. (1977). Nonprescription behavior therapies and other self-help treatments: a reply to Goldiamond. *American Psychologist*, 32, 178-179.

Rosen, G. M. (1978). Suggestions for an editorial policy on the review of self-help treatment books. *Behavior Therapy*, 9, 90.

Rosen, G. M. (1981). Guidelines for the review of do-it-yourself treatment books. *Contemporary Psychology*, 26, 189-191.

Rosen, G. M. (1987). Self-help treatment books and the commercialization of psychotherapy. *American Psychologist*, 42, 46-51.

Siegel, B. (1988). *Love, medicine & miracles: Lessons learned about self-healing from a surgeon's experience with exceptional patients*. New York: Harper & Row.

Simonds, W. (1992). *Women and self-help culture: Reading between the lines*. New Brunswick, NJ: Rutgers University Press.

Starker, S. (1986). Promises and prescriptions: self-help books in mental health and medicine. *American Journal Health Promotion*, 1, 19-24.

Starker, S. (1988). Do-it-yourself therapy: the prescription of self-help books by psychologists. *Psychotherapy*, 25, 142-146.

Starker, S. (1988). Psychologists and self-help books: attitudes and prescriptive practices of clinicians. *American Journal of Psychotherapy*, 3, 448-455.

Tannen, D. (1990). *You just don't understand: Women and men in conversation.* New York: Ballantine Books.

Tyson, R. (1949). It is respectable to publish interesting material for popular consumption? *American Psychologist, 535-536.*

Appendix 4

Glossary of Popular Psychology Terms

Addiction   A chronic pattern of behavior characterized by compulsive pleasure seeking. When the need is satisfied, there is a temporary period of euphoria, followed by feelings of extreme sadness and cravings. In the current vernacular, this term has been applied to persons "addicted" to alcohol, drugs, food, gambling, sex, shopping, and so forth.

Autosuggestion   A form of hypnosis developed by Emile Coué in the 1920's. Psychological symptoms were said to be the result of imagining oneself to be depressed or ill, and these problems could be solved if an individual could learn to imagine a happier self.

Behavior Modification	An outgrowth of B. F. Skinner's operant theory of behavior. Techniques which utilize reinforcement as a tool in altering a wide variety of human behaviors.
Bio-energetics	Form of therapy, associated with Alexander Lowen, which stresses the role of pleasure as a primary goal of psychotherapy.
Biofeedback	Behavior-modification techniques which involve providing persons with feedback regarding certain physiological functions like blood pressure or heart rate, so that they may gain some degree of control of these specific functions.
Codependency	Concept originally applied to the predicament facing the wives of alcoholics. Extended to cover a great many problems experienced by any person who has a relationship (e.g., spouse, child, friend, or employer) with anyone with a wide assortment of behavioral or emotional problems.
Denial	An earlier use developed by Sigmund Freud to describe one of the defense mechanisms of the ego. Additionally, the term is used in the "recovery movement" to describe an unconscious process that persons use

to block awareness of their own addictions or the addictions of those with whom they relate.

Dysfunctional family

Originating in family systems theory, this term is used extensively by recovery therapists to label an individual's family of orientation or family of procreation. Any family which displays emotional or physical abuse, disrespect, or in which members receive any negative messages.

Emmanuel Movement

Initiated in the early twentieth-century by ministers Elwood Worcester and Samuel McComb, this set of teachings combined principles of theology, medicine, and psychology. Aimed at differentiating "functional" problems, which were in the province of the ministry, from "organic" matters, which were directed to the medical community.

Encounter group

An aspect of humanistic psychology in the form of a group meeting spanning several hours to several days in which members engage in exercises aimed at maximizing self-realization.

Erhard Seminars Training (est)

As developed by layman Werner Erhard, this form of group training/

therapy centers on experience. A large number of persons meet together on two consecutive weekends and are led by a highly structured trainer who monitors strictly (e.g., whether a participant would be permitted to go to the bathroom).

Gestalt therapy

Originally proposed by Fritz Perls and his associates Ralph Hefferline and Paul Goodman, this form of psychotherapy is often characterized as confrontive and manipulative. Gestalt therapy centers on both immediacy and genuineness.

Inner child

A primary goal in the recovery process is said to be the healing of the "inner child." An ambiguous notion, having roots in wounds in need of repair and reclamation.

Lyceum lectures

Popular in the nineteenth-century, these presentations, often sponsored by the town lyceum, were given on a wide array of topics. Any member of the community could join the lyceum simply by paying an annual fee. The lyceum lecture was a vehicle for promoting numerous popular movements, including phrenology.

Mesmerism

Originally developed by Franz Mesmer, an eighteenth century Austrian physician who thought that illness was the result of problems in the flow of a "superfine fluid." Mesmer created a form of hypnosis so that persons could restore their physical health through the "re-enerization" of their bodies.

Mind Cure

A former nineteenth-century mesmerist, Phineas Quimby, began this form of therapy. His disciples included Mary Baker Eddy, the founder of Christian Science. Disease, perceived to be an error, was treated through efforts to alter the patient's ways of thinking. Patients were to speak of their troubles. Proponents of this approach stressed spirituality, relaxation training, and suggestion.

Neurasthenia

In his 1881 book, *American Nervousness*, neurologist George Beard used this term to describe physical and mental exhaustion presumedly caused by rapid social change.

New Age

Reflecting a combination of spiritualism and pseudoscience and encompassing a wide variety of approaches including subliminal learning, channeling, holistic health, astrology as well as forms of recovery.

New Thought   A religious movement, which began in the late nineteenth century and communicated messages of self-determination and individual power. A number of self-help authors identified with this tradition.

Open marriage   A marital system described by Nena and George O'Neill in their 1972 book. This form of marriage was to promote total individual freedom, including the right to maintain satellite sexual relationships.

Parent   A method of parent education form-
Effectiveness   ulated by Thomas Gordon, a
Training   disciple of Carl Rogers.   PET includes active listening, values clarification, and problem solving strategies.

Peak experience   Humanistic psychologist Abraham Maslow viewed this as a character-istic experience of self-actualizing persons.   Moments of awe and wonder in which an individual is absorbed totally.

Phrenology   A popular psychology disseminated by lecturers and pamphleteers from the nineteenth- to the early twen-tieth-century. Human personality is assessed through analyzing the shape (bumps) of a person's head.

Popular psychology

Material on human behavior which is intended for general consumption. Included are many books, articles, advice columns, radio and television programs, audiotapes as well as "tests."

Positive thinking

A form of pop religion and pop psychology contending that the key to happiness is simply thinking positively.

Primal scream

An aspect of primal therapy, which was developed by Arnold Janov. Primal screams may involve crying, shouting, cursing, and other forms of release of the pain of primal trauma.

Psychoanalysis

A school of psychology and psychotherapy formulated originally by Sigmund Freud. Emphasizes the importance of unconscious forces and early childhood experience in understanding human motivation. The therapeutic process centers on free association, transference, resistance, interpretation, and the working through of insights.

Reality therapy

Associated with William Glasser, this short-term therapy views people as self-determining. The main goal is to assist persons in meeting their needs more effectively.

Recovery   A movement developed and disseminated by numerous recovering addicts and professional therapists. Anyone who has ever had a problem with alcohol, drugs, love, food, or numerous other concerns or has had a relationship with anyone with such a problem is said to either be "in denial" or "in recovery."

Script   In Transactional Analysis, a plan developed early in life which directs an individual's life.

Self-actualization Concept associated with humanistic psychologists, Carl Rogers and Abraham Maslow, which describes people as potentially capable of spontaneity, a fresh approach to living, and personal growth.

Self-analysis   Originally developed by Sigmund Freud, who endeavored to analyze himself. Numerous popular psychology books have purported to teach the necessary methods to the lay reader.

Stress management Strategies used to minimize the negative impact of external factors and maximize the positive effect of such elements on one's physical and emotional health.

Subliminal audiotape

A tape, purporting to give signals inaudible to the human ear or which are to be played while an individual is asleep, which is said to influence attitudes or contribute to the learning of new material.

Support group

A group composed of persons who share a common problem and meet regularly to assist one another in coping with mutual life concerns.

Toxic shame

In the recovery literature, dys-functional families are said to create and reinforce such shame among their members. Toxic shame, toxic guilt, and toxic anger are frequently used as labels on an interchangeable basis.

Transactional Analysis

A form of counseling developed by Eric Berne, which centers on an analysis of communication trans-actions. Clients learn to analyze ego states, interpersonal games, and life scripts.

Twelve Steps

A set of mandates followed by most recovery groups. These principles derive from the tenets of Alcoholics Anonymous.

Author Index

Bold face italics indicate text page numbers

Subject Index

Bold face italics indicate text page numbers